What About Your Future?

Have You Lost Your Dream, Your Goal, Your Vision, Your Hope?

Dr. Eldon & Wanell Bollinger

ii

Unless otherwise indicated, the scripture quotations within this work are taken from many Bible sources including, but not limited to, the Living Bible, King James Version, New Living Translation, New American Standard Bible, and New International Version.

Eldon's proverbs and memory verses are scriptures and partial scriptures from many Bibles. The proverbs are sayings that I have written and gathered from everywhere over the last 50+ years. I love them and use them often. If any are yours, please let me know and I will gladly give you the credit. Thank you and God Bless.

BOOK EDITOR: BOB MILLER
One-Of-A-Kind Productions–For more information regarding this book or for acquiring additional copies, please visit our website...www.ooakp.com.

Because of the dynamic nature of the Internet, any URL links, Web or email addresses or other listings within this book may have changed since this book's publication and may no longer be valid. In addition, the opinions, ideas, or views expressed within this publication are solely those of the author and do not necessarily reflect the same of the publisher therefore, the publisher hereby disclaims any responsibility for them.

*"Before I formed thee in the belly
I knew thee; and before thou camest
forth out of the womb I sanctified thee,
and I ordained thee…"*
—Jeremiah 1:5 (KJV).

*"For I know the thoughts that I think toward
you, saith the LORD, thoughts of peace,
and not of evil, to give you an expected end"*
—Jeremiah 29:11 (KJV).

*"Call unto me, and I will answer
thee, and show thee great and mighty
things, which thou knowest not"*
—Jeremiah 33:3 (KJV).

Table Of Contents

What About Your Future?

x

CHAPTER 1

OUR THOUGHT LIFE

Proverbs 29:18 (KJV) says, *"Where there is no vision, the people perish."*

Proverbs 23:7 (KJV) says, *"For as a man thinketh in his heart, so is he."*

Proverbs 16:3 (KJV) says, *"Commit thy works unto the LORD, and thy thoughts shall be established."*

Proverbs 16:7 (ESV) tells us, *"When a man's ways please the LORD, he maketh even his enemies to be at peace with him."*

We are new creations, born in the image and likeness of God. Our old attitude of failure and defeat must be a thing of the past. We have been redeemed from Satan's evil dominion. We are constantly to be renewed in the spirit of our mind, having a fresh mental and spiritual attitude. We are to strip off the old nature and "put on" the new man. We must get rid of the old negative thoughts and put on a fresh new attitude. In other words, we must change our thought patterns and start dwelling on the good things God provides for us.

We are told in **2 Timothy 3:1 (KJV)**, *"This know also, that in the last days perilous times shall come."*

We are living in troubling times, and the world is indeed raging. However, the man of God does not need to fear or live in dread of what may happen when his heart is fixed on trusting God. Although we are safe in the arms of God, our thought process is critical of our success in this life. That is why the Scripture tells us to guard our thoughts, our mind. If we allow ourselves to continually think negative thoughts, our lives will gravitate toward negative things and negative people; our life will follow our thought process. Like a magnet, it will draw in what we constantly think about. If you always think positive, happy, joyful thoughts, you're going to be a happy, positive, joyful person, and you will attract other happy, upbeat, positive people. Remember: as a man think in his heart, so is he. If you want to live a blessed life, you must discover the power of your thoughts and your words.

Proverbs 10:22 (KJV), "The blessing of the Lord, it maketh rich, and he addeth no sorrow with it."

God is a God of blessing, and he loves and cares for his children. I want you to begin to expect and believe God for his blessings in your life. He tells us in his Word that all things work together for good to those who love God and are called according to his purpose. If you are born again, you are called according to his purpose, and all things will indeed work for your benefit when you are believe in and expect it to happen. Study the Word, feed upon God's Word and as your faith grows, begin to truly believe it, and expect God to answer each and every one of your prayers.

Our thought life affects our attitude in life. Our emotions will follow our attitude or thought life. We must first think happy thoughts, or we will never be happy. On the other hand, it is impossible to remain discouraged unless you first think discouraging thoughts. Most of success or failure in life begins in our minds and is influenced by what we allow ourselves to think about. Let's set our mind and heart upon the wonderful things of Almighty God and his Word. Victory and blessings will always follow. Remember, as a man thinketh in his heart, so is he.

You may not realize it, but we choose our thoughts. Satan will try to do that for you, but you don't have to let him. Your thought life is your choice. You decide what you will entertain in your mind. Simply because the devil plants a negative, discouraging thought in your mind doesn't mean you have to dwell on it and help it grow. Please realize that you can choose to cast it down or dismiss it from your mind. Let us choose to think about God's promises.

"Finally, brethren, whatsoever things are true, whatsoever things *are* honest, whatsoever things *are* just, whatsoever things *are* pure, whatsoever things *are* lovely, whatsoever things *are* of good report; if *there be* any virtue, and if *there be* any praise, think on these things"—**Philippians 4:8 (KJV)**, emphasis added.

You can choose to think positive thoughts. Fill your thoughts with God's Word, set your mind on things that edify, build up, encourage–these things make life a blessing. Your thought life regulates your attitude, your disposition, and your happiness or unhappiness; it thereby regulates and controls the affairs of your life.

Begin today to think about what you "Think About." Your life will never rise above your thought life. When you think positive, beautiful, and excellent thoughts, you will rise to that level. God tells us to meditate on his Word.

In **Psalm 1:1–3 (KJV)** it says, [1] *"Blessed is the man that walketh not in the counsel of the ungodly, nor standeth in the way of sinners, nor sitteth in the seat of the scornful.* [2] *But his delight in the law of the Lord: and in his law doth he meditate day and night.* [3] *He shall be like a tree planted by the river of water that bringeth forth his fruit in his season: his leaf also shall not wither; and whatsoever he doeth shall prosper."*

Meditate about things such as **Psalm 103:1–5 (KJV)**, [1] "Bless the LORD, O my soul, and all that is within me, *bless* his holy name. [2] Bless the LORD, O my soul, and forget not all his benefits, [3] who forgiveth all thine iniquities; who healeth all thy diseases; [4] who redeemeth thy life from destruction; who crowneth thee with loving kindness and tender mercies; [5] who satisfieth thy mouth with good *things; so that* thy youth is renewed like the eagle's."

[7] "Only be thou strong and very courageous, that thou mayest observe to do according to all the law, which Moses my servant commanded thee: turn not from it *to* the right hand or *to* the left, that thou mayest prosper whithersoever thou goest. [8] This book of the law shall not depart out of thy mouth; but thou shalt meditate therein day and night, that thou mayest observe to do according to all that is written therein: for then thou shalt make thy way prosperous, and then thou shalt have good success"—**Joshua 1:7–8 (KJV)**.

[1] "Praise ye the LORD. Blessed *is* the man *that* feareth the LORD, *that* delighteth greatly in his commandments. [2] His seed shall be mighty upon earth: the generation of the upright shall be blessed. [3] Wealth and riches *shall be* in his house: and his righteousness endureth forever"—**Psalm 112:1–3 (KJV)**, emphasis added.

"Beloved, I wish above all things that thou mayest prosper and be in health, even as thy soul prospereth"—**3 John 1:2 (KJV)**.

This is again something we are to do. We must continually keep our thoughts on God's good things, and our lives will eventually rise to that level. As a man thinketh in his heart, so is he!

Joel Osteen said, "If you will transform your mind, God will transform your life."

Author's note: I have written more than one hundred sheets of proverbs and memory verses, and I believe they can be a great encouragement and help in keeping our mind and thoughts on a positive and exciting plane. Because of that, I am inserting them in this book as I feel is necessary.

CHAPTER 2

PEACE IN THE TIME OF TROUBLE

ELDON'S PROVERBS AND MEMORY VERSES

PEACE 1:   REAL RICHES

1. Jesus said, 'I am leaving you a gift-peace of mind and heart'—**John 14:27 (LB)**

2. Great peace have they who keep thy law, and nothing shall offend them.

3. Wisdom from God gives a good long life, riches, and honor, pleasure and peace.

4. A fat purse will not compensate for a lien soul.

5. For length of days and long life and peace shall they add unto thee.

6. "Peace I leave with you, my peace I give unto you…"—**John 14:27 (KJV)**.

7. Live your life so your conscience will approve.

8. Learning to live peacefully is a lesson many people never learn.

9. He sends peace across your nation and fills your barns with plenty.

10. It's wrong to suppress laughter. It goes down and spreads to your hips.

11. They that seek the Lord shall not want any good thing: the eyes of the Lord are upon the righteous and his ears open to their cries. Let the peace of God keep your thoughts, your mind and your emotions.

12. A chapter a day helps keeps the devil away.

13. There is peace, though the world may be raging, in the shelter of his Word!

Eldon Bollinger

[1] *"This know also, that in the last days perilous times shall come.* [2] *For men shall be lovers of their own selves, covetous, boasters, proud, blasphemers, disobedient to parents, unthankful, unholy,* [3] *without natural affection, trucebreakers, false accusers, incontinent, fierce, despisers of those that are good,* [4] *traitors, heady, high minded, lovers of pleasures more than lovers of God;* [5] *having a form of godliness, but denying the power thereof: from such turn away"*—**2 Timothy 3:1–5 (KJV)**.

We are truly living in troubling times, and as sin abounds, the wrath of God cometh upon the children of disobedience. Although we are living in troubling times and the world is raging, the person who is born into the family of God does not need to be a part of it, nor to encounter the wrath of God as a result of what is happening in our world today. There can be peace though the world be raging, in the shelter of His Word, in his love.

When you are born again, you are redeemed out of Satan's dominion and into the family of God. You receive the nature of God, and God's nature is love. You put on the righteousness of God in Christ Jesus our Lord and you are sanctified, set apart unto God. At that time, you become a son or daughter of Almighty God, and you become an heir and a joint heir with Jesus Christ. You put on eternal life, and you are on your way to heaven.

Because of this, sin consciousness, guilt, doubt, and unbelief will lose their hold on you, and your faith will work. God's river of blessings will begin to flow into your life.

"For if by one man's [Adam] *offence, death reigned by one: much more they which receive abundance of grace and of the gift of righteousness shall reign in life by one Jesus Christ"*—**Romans 5:17 (KJV)**.

You see, you received the gift of righteousness when you were born into the family of God and you are now qualified to reign in life by Jesus Christ. God's river of blessings are now yours, by your faith.

ELDON'S PROVERBS AND MEMORY VERSES

FAITH 2:   REAL RICHES

1. Through faith, God's promises are mine.

2. The just shall live by faith.

3. Take the shield of faith.

4. Faith is a growing thing.

5. Faith is in the spirit, not in the mind.

6. Build up your most holy faith.

7. According to your faith be it unto you.

8. Not anything that is wrong, can ever turn out right.

9. There are no hopeless situations, only people who have lost hope.

10. Faith grows out of the knowledge of God's faithfulness.

11. Faith is the opposite of fear.

12. Grow your faith exceedingly.

Eldon Bollinger

CHAPTER 3

GOD'S RIVER OF BLESSINGS 1

"And we know that all things work together for good, to them that love God, to them who are called according to his purpose"–**Romans 8:28 (KJV)**.

"He that spared not his own Son, but delivered him up for us all, how shall He not with Him also freely give us all things"–**Romans 8:32 (KJV)**.

"Therefore let no man glory in man. For all things are yours"—**1 Corinthians 3:21 (KJV)**.

"Beloved, I wish above all things that thou mayest prosper and be in health, even as thy soul prospereth"—**3 John 1:2 (KJV)**.

ELDON'S PROVERBS AND MEMORY VERSES

FAITH 3:   REAL RICHES

1. Ask in faith nothing wavering.

2. Faith cometh by hearing the Word of God.

3. Whatsoever is not of faith is sin.

4. God is the author and finisher of our faith.

5. Without faith, it is impossible to please God.

6. The just shall live by their faith.

7. Faith is a growing thing.

8. Faith is in the spirit, not in the mind.

9. Stagger not at the promise of God through unbelief.

10. Take the shield of faith.

11. Most prayers are begging and pleading to God for things he has already given us.

12. Build up your most holy faith.

13. Feed your faith on God's Word.

Eldon Bollinger

Although God has freely given his children all things that pertain to life and godliness, most Christians never walk in the fullness of it because they don't know. They don't know they are victors and conquerors and overcomers. They don't know all the promises in God's

Word belongs to them. They don't know Satan is a defeated foe, and because of that, doubt and unbelief keep them defeated and whipped.

"The blessing of the Lord, it maketh rich, and he addeth no sorrow with it"—**Proverbs 10:22 (KJV)**.

"The fear of the wicked, it shall come upon him: but the desire of the righteous shall be granted"—**Proverbs 10:24 (KJV)**.

We all desire to be in the flow of God's blessings, and God makes it clear what is required of us. We must begin to observe and keep God's Word.

Matthew 7:24–25 (ASV) says, 24- *"Everyone therefore that heareth these words of mine, and doeth them, shall be likened unto a wise man, who built his house upon the rock;* 25-*and the rains descended, and the floods came and the winds blew, and beat upon that house: and it fell not, for it was founded upon the rock."*

Everyone who hears these sayings and acts upon them will be found to resemble a wise man who built his house upon the rock. The rock is doing the Word. He who does not do the Word ever builds upon a solid foundation.

Matthew 7:26 (KJV), 26- *"And everyone who hears these words and ignores them shall be likened unto a foolish man who built his house upon the sand."* The hearer must become a doer or else the entire structure he builds will be destroyed. Jesus illustrated that. He made us understand what acting on the Word really means.

ELDON'S PROVERBS AND MEMORY VERSES

FAITH 4:   REAL RICHES

1. We are put on this Earth not to see through one another but to see one another through.

2. All of the gifts and callings of God are yea, and amen to those who believe.

3. Ask in faith nothing wavering.

4. Now faith is the substance of things hoped for, the evidence of things not seen.

5. According to your faith, be it unto you.

6. Faith grows out of the knowledge of God's Word.

7. Not anything that is wrong can ever turn out right.

8. There are no hopeless situations, only people who have lost hope.

9. Through faith, God's promises are mine.

10. Faith is daring the soul to go beyond what the eye can see.

Eldon Bollinger

CHAPTER 4

THE WISE MAN VERSUS THE FOOLISH MAN

<u>The wise man is a doer of the Word.</u> The other hears but does not act upon it. He is a sense knowledge hearer. He hears the Word but he is not a doer. He responds to reason instead of the Word. His spiritual life is built on the sand. You can tell whether a man is building on the sand or on the rock by noticing whether he is practicing the Word or if he is acting on the Word.

James 1:22–25 (ASV) says, [22-]*"But be ye doers of the Word and not hearers only, deluding your own selves,* [23-]*for if anyone is a hearer of the Word and not a doer, he is like a natural man beholding his natural face in a mirror:* [24-]*for he beholds himself and goeth away, and straightway forgetteth what manner of man he was.* [25-]<u>*But he that looks into the perfect law of liberty, and so continueth, being not a hearer that forgetteth, but a doer that remembers, this man shall be blessed in his doings."*</u>

<u>It is the doer of the Word, the man who practices it, lives it, walks in it,</u> who builds it into his own life, whom God honors.

Examples of doing the Word:

Malachi 3:7–11 (KJV)

7 <u>Even from the days of your fathers ye are gone away from mine ordinances, and have not kept</u> *them*. <u>Return unto me, and I will return unto you, saith the LORD of hosts. But ye said, Wherein shall we return?</u>

8 <u>Will a man rob God? Yet ye have robbed me. But ye say, Wherein have we robbed thee? In tithes and offerings.</u>

9 <u>Ye</u> *are* <u>cursed with a curse: for ye have robbed me,</u> *even* <u>this whole nation.</u>

10 Bring ye all the tithes into the storehouse, that there may be meat in mine house, and prove me now herewith, saith the LORD of hosts, <u>if I will not open you the windows of heaven, and pour you out a blessing, that there shall not be room enough to receive it. God is saying, try me and see if I will not open the windows of heaven and pour you out you a blessing that there is not room enough to receive it.</u>

11 <u>And I will rebuke the devourer for your sakes, and he shall not destroy the fruits of your ground; neither shall your vine cast her fruit before the time in the field, saith the LORD of hosts.</u>

ELDON'S PROVERBS AND MEMORY VERSES

FAITH 6:   REAL RICHES

1. The purpose of this study, and my earnest desire, is to always be able to say, as Paul did to the Thessalonica, *"I thank God always for you, brethren, because your faith grows exceedingly and the [love] of each one of you abound toward each other"*—**2 Thessalonians 1:3**.

2. Faith is the opposite of fear.

   a) Through faith, Noah built an ark.

   b) Through faith, Enoch was translated.

   c) Through faith, the waters were rolled back.

   d) Through faith, the walls of Jericho came down.

   e) Through faith, all of God's promises are mine.

3. Feed your faith and your doubts will starve to death.

4. For we walk by faith and not by sight.

5. Jesus is the author and finisher of our faith.

6. Know ye that the Lord, he is God: and not we ourselves; we are his people.

7. The greatest act of faith is when a man decides he is not God.

8. Sorrow looks back. Worry looks around. Faith looks up.

9. Faith pleases God and brings his blessings.

Eldon Bollinger

God forgives, and his river of blessing comes back, making your life rich and full, and overflowing in every area with his love and blessing. As you become a doer of His Word, no good thing will he withhold from you.

"Give, and it shall be given unto you; good measure, pressed down, and shaken together, and running over, shall men give into your bosom. For with the same measure that ye mete withal it shall be measured to you again"—**Luke 6:38 (KJV).**

CHAPTER 5

THE FAITH WALK

ELDON'S PROVERBS AND MEMORY VERSES

FAITH 1:   REAL RICHES

1. Whatever is not of faith is sin.

2. Without faith, it is impossible to please God.

3. Faith cometh by hearing the Word of God.

4. Ask in faith nothing wavering.

5. God is the author and finisher of our faith.

6. Most prayers are begging and pleading with God for things he has already given us.

7. <u>The purpose of these Proverbs and my earnest desire is to always be able to say that as Paul did to the Thessalonians, I thank God always for you brethren, because your faith growth exceedingly and the love</u>

<u>of every one of you abounded towards each other more and more.</u>

8. All of the gifts and callings of God are yea and Amen to them that believe or have faith.

9. Now faith is the substance of things hoped for, the evidence of things not seen.

10. Feed your faith on God's Word.

11. We are not put on this earth to see through one another but to see one another through.

12. Stagger not at the promises of God through unbelief.

Eldon Bollinger

Hebrews 11:6 (KJV) states, <u>"But without faith it is impossible to please him!</u> For he that cometh to God must believe that he is, and that <u>he is a rewarder</u> of them that diligently seek him."

[1]-"Now faith is the substance of things hoped for, the evidence of things not seen. [2]-For by it the elders obtained a good report. [3]-Through faith we understand that the worlds were framed by the Word of God, so that things that are seen were not made with things that do appear"— **Hebrews 11:1–3 (KJV).**

[17]-*"For our light afflictions* [the problems that we face now], *which is but for a moment, worketh for us a far*

more exceeding and eternal weight of glory; [18] *while we look not at the things which are seen: but at the things which are not seen; for the things which are seen are temporal; but the things which are not seen are eternal"*—**2 Corinthians 4:17–18 (KJV).**

"(For we walk by faith, not by sight)"—**2 Corinthians 5:7 (KJV).**

"Now the just shall live by their faith..."—**Hebrews 10:38 (KJV).**

ELDON'S PROVERBS AND MEMORY VERSES

LOVE 1:   REAL RICHES

1. [7]"Beloved, let us love one another: for love is of God; and every one that loveth is born of God, and knoweth God. [8]He that loveth not knoweth not God; for God is love"—**1 John 4:7–8 (KJV).**

2. *"...and he that dwelleth in love dwelleth in God..."*— **1 John 4:16 (KJV).**

3. Love can bring healing to your life, your family, your world.

4. And the God of love and peace be with you.

5. Make love your way of life, then it cannot fail.

6. Let love rule your work, your play, your home, and your life.

7. The fruit of the Spirit is love.

8. Choose love's way every time.

9. The beautiful ministry of Jesus Christ was accomplished to give us joy and peace and love. He walked the rugged cobblestones to patiently teach us that in his Father's love was hope. His entire life was dedicated to this, and he viewed humanity with a burning desire to deliver them from their problems and burdens. He sought no earthly praise, and he ministered through love to all he met. And finally, looking down from the cross, he offered forgiveness and eternal life to all. What great love!

10. Love flowers must be watered often with tears and tender care.

His Banner Over Me Is Love

Eldon Bollinger

CHAPTER 6

THE LOVE LIFE

When one receives eternal life, he also receives the nature of God (a God of love).

Jesus said, *"a new commandment I give unto you, that ye love one another: as I have loved you, that ye also love one another"*—**John 13:34 (KJV)**.

"For God so loved the world, that He gave His only begotten Son, that whosoever believeth in Him should not perish, but have everlasting life"—**John 3:16 (KJV)**.

Love is of God and everyone that loveth is born of God.

[7] *"Beloved, let us love one another: for love is of God and everyone that loveth is born of God and knoweth God.* [8] *He that loveth not knoweth not God; for God is love"*—**1 John 4:7–8 (KJV)**.

God's Love Unlimited

Man has had an abundance of spiritual death. It reigned over him. It was his master. All the sins and crimes and wars have grown out of that awful thing called spiritual death. It was the very nature of Satan. **Romans 5:12–21**, is God's commentary on it. It is called the law of sin and of death **Romans 8:2–3**. Even the 10 Commandments are called the law of sin. This law of sin was manifest in the human family.

<u>Eternal life is the nature of God</u>, and spiritual death is the nature of Satan, see **2 Peter 1:4**.

There is a combat between life and death, between God's nature and Satan's nature in man. Just as spiritual death swallowed the human race, so God is going to give eternal life in such abundance that it will swallow up death. *"For indeed we that are in this tabernacle [body] do groan, being burdened; not for that we would be unclothed, but that we would be clothed upon, that which is mortal may be swallowed up of life"*—**2 Corinthians 5:4 (ASV)**.

This word life is Zoe. Way translates it, drowned in the sea of life, showing the abundance of life. There is in the world today an abundance of sickness. There is the very fullness of Satan. It is apparent everywhere. Men are filled with the devil.

A new order is coming, however. Man is to be filled with God, filled with his nature, his life, his being–to be like him, swayed by him, and ruled by him.

ELDON'S PROVERBS AND MEMORY VERSES

LOVE 2:   REAL RICHES

1. There are three things that remain: faith, hope, and love–and the greatest of these is love.

2. Love should not be thought of as something we get but something we give.

3. Perfect love casteth out fear.

4. Owe no man anything but to love one another: for he that loveth another hath fulfilled God's law.

5. Beloved, if God so loved us, we ought also to love one another.

6. See that ye love one another with a pure and fervent heart.

7. Bless those who that mistreat you, be kind to those who curse you, and be good to those who hate you, pray for those who spitefully use you. This is love in action.

8. Though I have the gift of prophecy, and I understand all things, and though I have all faith, so that I can move mountains and have not love, I am nothing.

9. By this shall all men know that we are Christians, if we have loved one to another.

10. A friend is one who knows all about you and loves you anyway.

11. Love is a fruit for all seasons.

12. Love forgets mistakes.

13. A bit of fragrance always clings to the hand that gives out love flowers.

Eldon Bollinger

CHAPTER 7

OUR LOVE NATURE

God is love. **1 John 4:8** shows us that man is to be filled with agape, the new kind of love. It has never been taught. The church has never majored in its teachings and creeds.

Can you conceive of a body of believers filled with the life and nature of God?

We understand **Colossians 2:9–10 (ASV)**, [9-]*"For in Him dwelleth all the fullness of the Godhead bodily;* [10-]*and in Him ye are made full who is the head of all principalities and powers."*

We are made full of the nature of God, full of God. That explains **John 1:16 (NASV)**, *"For of his fullness have we all received, and grace upon grace."*

Of his abundant nature, abundant life, have we all received. That means that we have received of his love life (see **1 John 4:16***) and we know and have believed the love which God hath in our case. God is love. He that abides in love abides in God and God abides in him we* *abide or live in our daily walk in the life and nature of God. The nature of God dominates us, rules us. We live in the realm of love. The love nature dominates our lives just as Jesus in his earth walk lived in the realm of love,* see **1 John 4:17–18**.

Now we have been translated out of the kingdom of darkness [of Satan's nature] *into the kingdom of the Son of his love,* see **Colossians 1:13**.

That love nature of God has swallowed up, dominated us so we act like lovers, we speak like lovers, and our conduct is governed by this nature of God, this new nature given to man. Can you visualize a man living in God, walking in God? Just as you walk in the early morning heavy fog that shrouds your clothes and drips from your hat, you are walking in God until you are saturated with God's love, until love drips from your words. Your entire being is saturated in love.

We can understand **1 John 4:6–7 (KJV)**, [6] *"We are of God: he that knoweth God heareth us; he that is not of God heareth not us. Hereby know we the spirit of truth, and the spirit of error.* [7] *Beloved, let us love one another: for love is of God; and every one that loveth is born of God, and knoweth God."*

The test of the new birth is this love life. How beautiful it would be if we were actually swallowed up of love. That is what it means–swallowed up of life–and life is love. It would solve the homeless problem, wouldn't it? There would be no quarrelling or bitterness. What a heavenly atmosphere the children would grow up in; they would never hear an unkind word or a bitter criticism.

You can read **1 John 5:13 (ASV)**; *"These things have I written unto you, that you may know that you have eternal life, even unto you that believe on the name of the Son of God."* You could read it this way; we know we have received the nature of God, this love life. We know we are in the love family. The abundance of his life dominates us. We are ruled by the abundance of God from **Hebrews 11:3 (KJV)**; *"...we understand that the worlds were framed by the Word of God..."* God is not only a love God, he is a faith God. We have in us this faith, God's nature, so faith becomes an unconscious fact in our lives, just as it was in Jesus' life.

Jesus has no consciousness of the need or lack of faith. He has no consciousness of the need or lack of love. He lived in the realm of life. He had this life in abundance. He had love and faith in abundance. This throws new light upon the sentence in **James 1:22 (ASV)**, "<u>But be ye doers of the Word and not hearers only, deluding your own selves.</u>"

CHAPTER 8

DOERS OF LOVE AND FAITH

The Word is love expressed. Love has spoken, and we have a record of it. <u>I become a doer of the Word, then I become a doer of love. I become a doer of faith. I become a doer of this abundant life that is in me. I am living it, letting it loose in me. It lives in me and rules me.</u> I am not deceiving myself now with mere empty profession because I assent to a creed or the doctrine of a church. This means very little to the world and to the Father. But now that Word has become part of my very being. It is building into me the love nature of the Father.

Jesus said in **Matthew 7:24 (ASV)**, *"Everyone therefore that heareth these words of mine and doeth them, shall be likened unto a wise man that built his house up on the rock."* Then he contrasted it in verse 26 with the foolish man who didn't do the Word, and built his house upon the sand. It is the doer of love, the doer of faith who is the doer of the Word.

"If ye know that he is righteous, ye know that every one that doeth righteousness is born of him"—**1 John 2:29 (KJV)**.

What is righteousness? It is acting in the realm of Love. It is doing love, as Jesus did love. Love gives us a holy boldness, as is mentioned in **1 John 4:18 (ASV)**, *"There is no fear in love: but perfect love casteth out fear…"*

ELDON'S PROVERBS AND MEMORY VERSES

LOVE 3:   REAL RICHES

1. Show love and kindness to unkind people, they probably need it most of all.

2. Unconditional love is loving without conditions.

3. It doesn't take a dictionary to learn the language of love.

4. Dear friends: let us practice loving each other, for love comes from God, and those who are loving and kind show they are the children of God. If a person isn't loving and kind it shows he doesn't know God, for God is love. When God lives in us, his love within us grows and becomes strong. If anyone says, "I love God," but keeps hating his brother, he is a liar; for if he doesn't love his brother, whom he can see, how can he love God, whom he has never seen?

5. Jesus said, "A new commandment I give unto you, that ye love one another: even as I have loved you, that ye also love one another"—**John 13:34 (KJV)**.

6. When one receives eternal life, he also receives the nature of God [a God of love].

7. This I pray: that your love may abound yet more and more.

8. Faultfinding disappears where love is growing.

9. Little children, <u>let us stop just saying we love people; let us really love them and show it by our actions.</u>

10. **LOVE NEVER FAILS.**

Eldon Bollinger

CHAPTER 9

LOVE MAKES US MASTERS

Love lets us into the throne room and the very presence of the Father, see **Hebrews 4:16**. Love makes us masters over disease and over lack, weakness, and failure. Love makes us conquerors. Letting love loose in me is letting God loose in me, for God is love. **Ephesians 3:19 (ASV)** says, *"And to know the love of Christ, which passeth knowledge, that ye may be filled with all the fulness of God."*

Knowledge here is sense knowledge. This Christ's love is the Father's love. It is the abundance of the nature of the Father. It is the abundance of God unveiled in Christ Jesus. The Scripture says that we may know this love; that is, speaking it, entering into it. We are also to be filled unto all the fullness of God according to **1 John 3:14–21**. That belongs to us; it is our inheritance. That is one of the things **Ephesians 1:3 (ASV)** brings to us, *"Blessed be the God and Father of our Lord Jesus Christ, who hath blessed us with every spiritual blessing in the heavenly places in Christ."*

He has filled us with the fullness of himself. As the air is saturated with moisture, so your spirit and body are saturated with God. You have received the gift of grace, which means the unveiling of the Father's very purpose in you in such abundance that people are affected by what you say. You are rooted and grounded in love. Men are affected by it; selfishness shrinks and shrivels in the presence of this love life in you.

You are living **Ephesians 4:13 (ASV)**, *"Till we all attain unto the unity of the faith, and of the knowledge of the Son of God, unto a full-grown man, unto the measure of the fullness of Christ."* This is the substance of God. This is the abundance of life. This is being rooted and grounded in the love life, the love nature of the Father himself. We can now understand **Romans 15:1–2 (ASV)**, *"We that are strong ought to bear the infirmities of the weak and not to please ourselves; let each of us please his neighbor according to that which is edifying."* Then He illustrates it in **Romans 15:3 (ASV)**, *"for even Christ also pleased not himself."*

The new self that has come unto us is a Jesus self, a love self. It is an eternal-life self, a God-ruled, God-dominated self. We are taking over the overload of man around us. We are taking Jesus' place in the earth; you are bearing man's infirmities instead of finding fault with them and criticizing them. Jesus is thrilled by your conduct toward man, and I can hear him whisper, "Father, aren't we glad we made the sacrifice? See how they are responding to your love nature and your love call?"

How wonderful is **Ephesians 5:18–19 (KJV)**? [18]-*"Be not drunk with wine, wherein excess, but be filled with the spirit;* [19]-*speaking one to another in psalms and hymns and spiritual songs, singing and making melody in your heart to the Lord."*

Then the twentieth & twenty-first verses becomes a reality, [20]-*"Giving thanks always for all things in the name of our Lord Jesus Christ* [to God, the Father]; [21]-*subjecting yourself one to another in the fear of Christ."* Now we move up into the realm into which we have been translated, the kingdom of the son of his love. **Colossians 1:13 (KJV)** tells us we are living in that new realm, *"Who hath delivered us from the power of darkness, and hath translated us into the kingdom of his dear Son."*

ELDON'S PROVERBS AND MEMORY VERSES

LOVE 4:   REAL RICHES

1. Love sees and understands what no eye can see; love hears and understands what no ear can hear.

2. Riches and this world's possessions cannot replace love.

3. Love forgets mistakes; nagging over them separates the best of friends.

4. Love not the world or the things in the world, but love people and God.

5. The value of life increases greatly when love appears.

6. Love mends and heals; selfishness tears apart.

7. The problems of life are diminished greatly when you are loved.

8. God's love always gives and does not demand love in return.

9. When you have nothing else to give, give love. It is the best gift of all.

10. Love your enemies, and do good to those who spitefully use you.

11. If you really want God's smile of approval, forgive and love those who have hurt you.

12. A home where love abounds is always abounding in joy, peace, laughter, and happiness.

Eldon Bollinger

CHAPTER 10

A BRANCH OF THE VINE

Men recognize us as branches of the vine, and they say, "Notice the wonderful fruitage, the great clusters of ripened fruit that are in the lives of those men and women." **John 15:5 (KJV)** adds, *"I am the vine, ye are the branches: he that abideth in me, and I in him, the same bringeth forth much fruit: for without me ye can do nothing."* It is love fruit. It is the fruit of the abundant life. The master has gained the ascendancy now. Jesus is crowned as Lord of the heart, just as we get it in **1 Peter 3:15 (KJV),** *"But sanctify the Lord God in your hearts: and be ready always to give an answer to every man that asketh you a reason of the hope that is in you with meekness and fear."*

Sanctify means to set apart, as in to set apart Christ as Lord in your heart. His lordship is the lordship of love. **Colossians 2:6–7 (NASV)** makes it even more manifest, *"Therefore you who received Jesus Christ as Lord, so walk in him, rooted and built up in him, and established in your faith, even as ye were taught, abounding with thanksgiving."* Here is full growth. Here is the abundant life taking us over, crowning Jesus as the very Lord of our being so that his heart is filled with joy over us.

24- "For our comely parts have no need: but God hath tempered the body together, having given more abundant honor to that part which lacked. 25-That there should be no schism in the body; but that the members should have the same care one for another. 26-And whether one member suffer, all the members suffer with it; or one member be honored, all the members rejoice with it"—**1 Corinthians 12:24–26 (KJV).**

Here is a demonstration of love. The Father knew there would be some members of the body who would never receive any special honor or glory from man, so he glorifies them himself, that there should be no schism in the body, but that the members should have the same care one for another. And when one member suffers, all members suffer; and whether one member is honored, all the members rejoice. This is where love has actually gained the ascendancy. **1 Corinthians 10:24 (KJV)** has become a reality; *"Let no man seek his own, but every man another's wealth."*

In **1 Corinthians 10:33 (ASV)** Paul says, *"Even as I also please all men in all things, not seeking mine own profit, that the profit of the many that they may be saved."* **Colossians 3:16 (KJV)** adds, *"Let the Word of Christ dwell in you richly in all wisdom; teaching and admonishing one another in psalms and hymns and spiritual songs, singing with grace in your hearts to the Lord."*

Now our words are love filled, and this is abundant life. This is God actually being let loose in us!

ELDON'S PROVERBS AND MEMORY VERSES

LOVE 5:   REAL RICHES

1. Dear children: let us practice loving each other, for love comes from God and those who are loving and kind show they are the children of God, and they are getting to know him better. <u>Now our words are love–filled; this is abundant life. This is God actually being let loose in us!</u>

2. When you perfect your love for others, you are also perfecting your love of God.

3. Faultfinding disappears where love is growing.

4. Love mends; selfishness tears apart.

5. Pride gives advice; love lends a hand.

6. Love prevails when everything else fails.

7. Love not the world nor the things in the world; love people and love God.

8. We are commanded by God's Word to love one another.

9. Riches of this world cannot replace love.

10. The value of life increases greatly when love appears.

11. The darkness in our lives disappears, as we love, as God commanded.

12. If anyone says "I love God" but keeps on hating his brother, he is a liar, for if he doesn't love his brother, who he can see, how can he love God, who can never be seen?

Eldon Bollinger

CHAPTER 11

THE NEW CREATION

The person that is not in Christ is, at this time, separated from Christ, alienated and strangers from the covenant of promise, having no hope and without God in the world. They are separated from Christ, and Christ alone has eternal life. *Jesus came to this earth that we might have life and have it more abundantly,* see **John 10:10**.

Hebrews 9:12 (NKJV), *"Not with the blood of goats and the caves, but with His own blood He entered the Most Holy Place once for all, having obtained eternal redemption."* Redeemed from Satan's domain–poverty, sickness and spiritual death having no hope!

In Christ we have our redemption from Satan's domain. It is an eternal redemption. It is available now. **Ephesians 1:7 (ASV)** states, *"In whom we have our redemption through His blood, the [forgiveness] of our sins according to the riches of his grace."*

We have the redemption (forgiveness) of our trespasses. The word forgiveness seems inadequate. Remission

<u>means to wipe out everything we have done up to the time we come to Christ.</u> No matter how much Satan has trapped us in his snares, the minute we are born again we stand before God as new creations, without the smell of our past life upon our spirits. According to **2 Corinthians 5:21**, the instant we are born again we become the righteousness of God in Christ. The instant we become the righteousness of God, Satan's dominion over us is broken. Instead of being slaves to Satan, we become the masters of circumstances. Instead of circumstances lording over us, we become their master.

This means the days of weakness and failure are ended for the man who knows the Word and dares to act upon it. According to **2 Corinthians 5:17–18 (ASV)**,
[17]-*"Wherefore if any man is in Christ he is a new creation; old things are passed away; behold they are become new,* [18]-*and all things are of God who has reconciled us to himself in Jesus Christ…"*

Notice carefully if any man is in Christ. When we accept Christ as our Savior and confess to him as our Lord, we become a branch of the vine. Jesus said, *"I am the vine and ye are the branches,"* we become utterly one with Christ—**John 15:5 (KJV)**.

2 Peter 1:4 (KJV) tells us we "become partakers of the divine nature, having escaped the corruption that is in the world…" because of Adam's transgression. That corruption is Spiritual death; the escape is eternal life.

"I am come that they might have life and have it more abundantly"—(**John 10:10**).

1 John 5:13 is reality for the new creation: *"These things have I written unto you that you may know that you have eternal life, even to you that believe on his name."*

The instant you believe and confess Jesus as your Lord, you become a possessor of the Father's nature. *You become a child of God, just like Jesus did when he was upon the earth.* <u>You may not have developed; you may not have grown in grace and in the knowledge of the Word; you may not have taken advantage of your privileges as a son, but you are a son, and an heir of God and a joint heir with Christ, until we recognize that we are new creations, the very sons and daughters of God, we will never take our place.</u>

2 Corinthians 5:17 (ASV) says, *"Wherefore if any man is in Christ, he is a new creation."* In the mind of God, the old man has stopped being. A new man has taken his place, and **Ephesians 4:23–24** has become a living, thrilling reality.

CHAPTER 12

THE NATURAL MAN

"But the natural man receiveth not the things of the Spirit of God: for they are foolishness unto him: neither can he know them because they are spiritually discerned"—**1 Corinthians 2:14 (KJV)**. You must be born again–become a new creation!

Natural man that has not been born again cannot understand the scriptures for they seem like foolishness to him. **Romans 10:9–10** tells us how to be saved or born again.

John 3:16 (KJV) said, *"For God so loved the world, that he gave his only begotten Son, that whosoever believeth in him should not perish, but have everlasting life."* **Romans 3:23 (KJV)** adds, *"For all have sinned, and came short of the glory of God."* **Romans 6:23 (KJV)**, *"For the wages of sin is death; but the gift of God is eternal life through Jesus Christ our Lord."*

Romans 10:9–10 (KJV) it tells us, [9] *"That if thou shall confess with my mouth the Lord Jesus Christ, and shalt believe in thine heart that God hath raised Him from the* *dead, thou shall be saved.* [10-]*For with the heart men believeth unto righteousness and with the mouth confession is made unto salvation."* Lastly, **Romans 10:13 (KJV)** states, *"For whosoever shall call upon the name of the Lord shall be saved."*

CHAPTER 13

THE PRAYER OF SALVATION

We are now actually new creations in Christ Jesus. According to **2 Corinthians 5:17 (KJV)**, *"Wherefore, if any man be in Christ, he is a new creature* [creation]*: old things are passed away; behold all things are become new."* He is a new creation, a new species. He has received into his spirit the life and nature of God.

The new creation is the product of God. He is created in Christ Jesus. He is born from above. He is born of the Holy Spirit through the Word of God, and this new creation stands uncondemned and reconciled before God our Father.

Corinthians 5:21 (ASV) states it clearly, *"Him who knew no sin* [Jesus] *was made to be sin on our behalf; that we might become the righteousness of God in him."* The moment we become new creations, we become the righteousness of God. We are at that moment sons and daughters of God. **1 John 3:2 (KJV)**, *"Beloved, now are we the sons of God, and it does not yet appear what we shall be; but we know that, when he shall appear, we shall be like him. For we shall see him as he is."* **1 John 5:13**

(KJV) also says, *"These things have I written unto you that believe on the name of the Son of God; that ye may know that ye have eternal life, and that ye may believe on the name of the Son of God."*

ELDON'S PROVERBS AND MEMORY VERSES

HAPPINESS 1:   REAL RICHES

1. Do not expect someone else to open the door to happiness for you; you must do it yourself. You alone have the key, so use it.

2. It isn't our position but our disposition that makes us happy or unhappy.

3. Do not seek happiness, seek to give happiness, and your happiness is assured.

4. God's blessing is our greatest wealth; all our work adds nothing to it. *Happiness comes from knowing and serving our Lord.*

5. Laugh at yourself now and then.

6. Happiness is like perfume; you can't give it away without getting a little on yourself.

7. Sow seeds of love, friendship, and happiness; you will reap what you sow.

8. You can exchange wearisome hours for hours of joy and delight by developing your love of others.

9. You can be as happy as you make up your mind to be.

10. Delight yourself in the Lord.

11. Man should eat, drink, and enjoy the good of all his labor, it is a gift from God to enjoy your work and to accept your lot in life.

12. *"He that is of a merry heart hath a continual feast"* —**Proverbs 15:15 (KJV)**.

Eldon Bollinger

CHAPTER 14

GOD'S RIVER OF BLESSINGS 2

<u>Our world is full of Christians who have been born into the family of God but have never gone on to obtain and enjoy the fullness of all God has for his children or his plans for their lives.</u>

The purpose of this book is to excite you and to build within you the enthusiasm, the joy, and the hope of all that belongs to you in Christ Jesus our Lord.

"Beloved, I wish above all things that thou mayest prosper and be in health, even as thy soul prospereth"—**3 John 1:2 (ASV)**. Prospering financially and physically is very much related to our soul prospering or to our spiritual growth.

God's abundance is being released for you

2 Peter 1:1–11 (NLT)
[1] *This letter is from Simon Peter, a slave and apostle of Jesus Christ. I am writing to you who share the same precious faith we have. This faith was given to you*

because of the justice and fairness of Jesus Christ, our God and Savior.

2 *May God give you more and more grace and peace as you grow in your knowledge of God and Jesus our Lord*

3 *By his divine power, God has given us everything we need for living a godly life. We have received all of this by coming to know him, the one who called us to himself by means of his marvelous glory and excellence.*

4 *And because of his glory and excellence, he has given us great and precious promises. These are the promises that enable you to share his divine nature and escape the world's corruption caused by human desires.*

5 *In view of all this, make every effort to respond to God's promises. Supplement your faith with a generous provision of moral excellence, and moral excellence with knowledge,*

6 *and knowledge with self-control, and self-control with patient endurance, and patient endurance with godliness,*

7 *and godliness with brotherly affection, and brotherly affection with love for everyone.*

8 *The more you grow like this, the more productive and useful you will be in your knowledge of our Lord Jesus Christ.*

9 *But those who fail to develop in this way are short sighted or blind, forgetting that they have been cleansed from their old sins.*

10 *So, dear brothers and sisters, work hard to prove that you really are among those God has called and chosen. Do these things, and you will never fall away.*

11 Then God will give you a grand entrance into the eternal Kingdom of our Lord and Savior Jesus Christ.

My goal is to encourage you and to speak faith into your life, to let you know that although we are in perilous times, God is still in control. His promises tell us all is well for the man or woman of God who seeks first the kingdom of God and his righteousness. He wants to let you know your future is bright!

What the news media may be telling us is that we're in a recession, that many have lost their jobs or their homes or both, and that lots of people are living below the poverty level, but that is not what God intends for his people. **Psalm 84:11 (KJV)** says, *"...No good thing will God withhold from those who walk uprightly."*

When your life pleases God and you daily seek the things of God, when your efforts are to help people and to build the kingdom of God and you live a life of integrity, God's favor and blessings will flow into your life.

God is saying, "I will not withhold the things you need, such as wisdom, joy, peace, love, victory, the council of God, the right connections, or your creative ability to make good in any work situation." God knew you before you were born; he made you in his likeness and created you to be a success in this life.

The man of God who seeks first the kingdom of God and his righteousness in every situation may be in a desert area situation at this time, but God will cause this desert situation to become like a Garden of Eden! The words "no good thing" means nothing good will God withhold. Remember, **Deuteronomy 28:1–2** tell us that all these blessings shall come on us and overtake us because we observe and keep God's Word. This is God's will for your life!

<u>If I can inspire your faith and get you to understand that God is our heavenly Father</u> who cares lovingly about every detail of our lives, you will rise to new heights of faith, and your river of blessings will flow!

2 Chronicles 7:14 (KJV), *"If my people, which are called by my name, shall humble themselves, and pray, and seek my face, and turn from their wicked ways, then will I hear from heaven, and will forgive their sin, and will heal their land."*

God will heal and restore any people or land that turn to him with all their hearts and obey his Word. God brought the children of Israel out of two hundred years of captivity in Egypt and across the desert, and he guaranteed them a promised land that flows with milk and honey. He also promised he would take care of them and drive the inhabitants of the land out. <u>However, they would not believe, they gave a negative confession, so they wandered in the wilderness until all adults twenty years and older had died. Doubt, fear, and disbelief robbed them of what God had promised them.</u>

God has given us a Book of Promises and tells us every promise in the book belongs to us. He also said he watches over his Word to perform it in our lives, and he is now telling us that no good thing will he withhold from us if we walk in his ways.

Can it possibly be that any of us will refuse to believe God and make a negative confession about what he has promised? If we do, we will walk in the "wilderness of life" the rest of our lives. No, no, no–none of us are going to do that! We are going to believe God, are we are going to walk by faith and not by sight, and we are going to observe and follow God's Word all the days of our lives.

When the young children of Israel came out of the wilderness, Moses was old and God did not allow him to go into the Promised Land. He gave that job to Joshua. Listen carefully to what God told Joshua as he took command of the children of Israel and was instructed to take them across the muddy Jordan into the promised land.

Joshua 1:1–2 (KJV)
1 *Now after the death of Moses the servant of the LORD it came to pass, that the LORD spoke unto Joshua the son of Nun, Moses' minister, saying,*
2 *'Moses my servant is dead; now therefore arise, go over this Jordan, thou, and all this people, unto the land which I do give to them, even to the children of Israel.'*

Joshua 2:24 (NKJV), "*And they said to Joshua, "Truly the LORD has delivered all the land into our hands, for* *indeed all the inhabitants of the country are fainthearted because of us."*

CHAPTER 15

GOD SAID TO JOSHUA

Joshua1:6–9 (KJV)

6 Be strong and of a good courage: for unto this people shall thou divide for an inheritance the land, which I sware unto their fathers to give them.

7 Only be thou strong and very courageous, that thou mayest observe to do according to all the law, which Moses my servant commanded thee: turn not from it *to* the right hand or *to* the left, that thou mayest prosper whithersoever thou goest.

8 This book of the law shall not depart out of thy mouth; but thou shalt meditate therein day and night, that thou mayest observe to do according to all that is written therein: for then thou shalt make thy way prosperous, and then thou shalt have good success.

9 Have not I commanded thee? Be strong and of a good courage; be not afraid, neither be thou dismayed: for the LORD thy God is with thee whithersoever thou goest.

The economic downturn has affected most everyone. Many have been through great struggles, many have lost their jobs and savings–you may have lost your home–your ability to get along with others has been strained, and we have all been tested severely!

Those who have their trust and faith in God will rise to the top in such times. <u>Understanding that God is looking after you personally and cares about everything that affects your life becomes vitally important.</u>

CHAPTER 16

GOD'S RIVER OF BLESSINGS 3

Turn your faith loose, study and feed upon God's Word. Remember, "Your best is yet to come," and your faith can move any mountain. **Mark 11:23** tells us how to get rid of any mountain of problems. He also tells us to speak to the mountain, and whatsoever we say will come to pass. Do you believe God and his Word? He watches over his Word to perform it. Get bold in your faith walk, for we walk by faith and not by sight. If God said it, I believe it, and I will act upon it!

The blessing and favor of the Lord makes it rich, and he adds no sorrow to it. God wants to restore you, wants to make your life a blessing, so it's time to trust and believe God and to build your determination to seek God's best. <u>No, nothing is as important as finding the favor of God in your life.</u>

For the man of God who fully studies and obeys God's Word, it doesn't matter what's happening to the world economy. It doesn't really matter what the stock market is doing. The only thing that really matters is whether we are pleasing God with our lives and have we obtained God's favor.

Deuteronomy 28:1–15

[1] *If you fully obey the LORD your God and carefully follow all his commands I give you today, the LORD your God will set you high above all the nations on earth.*

[2] *All these blessings will come on you and accompany you if you obey the LORD your God:*

[3] *You will be blessed in the city and blessed in the country.*

[4] *The fruit of your womb will be blessed, and the crops of your land and the young of your livestock–the calves of your herds and the lambs of your flocks.*

[5] *Your basket and your kneading trough will be blessed.*

[6] *You will be blessed when you come in and blessed when you go out.*

[7] *The LORD will grant that the enemies who rise up against you will be defeated before you. They will come at you from one direction but flee from you in seven.*

[8] *The LORD will send a blessing on your barns and on everything you put your hand to. The LORD your God will bless you in the land he is giving you.*

[9] *The LORD will establish you as his holy people, as he promised you on oath, if you keep the commands of the LORD your God and walk in obedience to him.*

[10] *Then all the peoples on earth will see that you are called by the name of the LORD, and they will fear.*

[11] *The LORD will grant you abundant prosperity–in the fruit of your womb, the young of your livestock and the*

crops of your ground—in the land he swore to your ancestors to give you.

12 The LORD will open the heavens, the storehouse of his bounty, to send rain on your land in season and to bless all the work of your hands. You will lend to many nations but will borrow from none.

13 The LORD will make you the head, not the tail. If you pay attention to the commands of the LORD your God that I give you this day and carefully follow them, you will always be at the top, never at the bottom.

14 Do not turn aside from any of the commands I give you today, to the right or to the left, following other gods and serving them.

15 However, if you do not obey the LORD your God and do not carefully follow all his commands and decrees I am giving you today, all these curses will come on you and overtake you.

This tells us the key to receiving the overflow of God's blessing into our lives. These Scriptures are promises made in the old covenant, made to the children of Israel, and they failed miserably in keeping God's Word. As a result, they lost everything instead of being blessed beyond expression.

The promises made in the old covenant apply to us today by our faith and the same rules apply—if we learn his and follow his Word, the blessings will flow! However, if we are unconcerned and do not become doers of God's Word, the same problems that happened to the children of Israel will happen to us.

CHAPTER 17

GOD'S PROMISED BLESSING

"If you fully obey the LORD your God and carefully follow all his commands I give you today, the LORD your God will set you on high above all the nations on earth. All these blessings will come upon you and overtake you if you obey the LORD your God"—**Deuteronomy 28:1–2 (NIV).**

ELDON'S PROVERBS AND MEMORY VERSES

GOD'S WORD 2: REAL RICHES

1. Trust God's Word completely, for when you do, every promised blessing comes to you.

2. A regular diet of God's Word will add long life and peace to you.

3. Clothe yourself in God's promises.

4. The Word of the Lord produces rich rewards.

5. When our ways and deeds are guided by God's Word, God's blessings will always follow.

6. Listen, observe, hear, digest, and do God's Word.

7. God's Word is alive and active it will produce in your life your hearts desires.

8. God's Word may seem unreal, but it is more real than life itself–it produces life and radiant health.

9. God's Word produces in my life, healing, radiant health, and life more abundant, full of joy and peace, and richness to my life beyond most minds' ability to comprehend. It produces a song in my heart and on my lips that never goes away. It is a peace that endures and overcomes any trial and is a joy the world cannot know and cannot take away.

10. Feed on God's Word.

Eldon Bollinger

Listed below are the results of not listening to God's Word or not becoming doers of the Word!

Jeremiah 25:8–11 (NIV)
8 *Therefore the LORD Almighty says this: 'Because you have not listened to my Words,*
9 *I will summon all the peoples of the north and my servant Nebuchadnezzar king of Babylon,' declares the LORD, 'and I will bring them against this land and its*

inhabitants and against all the surrounding nations. I will completely destroy them and make them an object of horror and scorn, and an everlasting ruin.

[10] *I will banish from them the sounds of joy and gladness, the voices of bride and bridegroom, the sound of millstones and the light of the lamp.*

[11] *This whole country will become a desolate wasteland, and these nations will serve the king of Babylon seventy years.*

In A.D.70, fewer than fifty years after Christ's prophecy, the Roman army besieged Jerusalem, killing more than one million inhabitants. The Roman legions leveled the city of Jerusalem, fulfilling Christ's prophecy that they "shall not leave in thee one stone upon another"—**Luke 19:44 (KJV)**, and the awful cry of the people, "Let him be crucified and his blood be on us, and on our children," had its tragic fulfillment, see **Matthew 27:25**.

CHAPTER 18

ISRAEL SCATTERED THROUGHOUT THE WORLD

[16]-*"Moreover the Word of the Lord came unto me, saying, *[17]-*Son of man, when the house of Israel dwelt in their own land, they defiled it by their own way and by their doings: their way was before me as the uncleanness of a removed woman. *[18]-*Wherefore I poured my fury upon them for the blood that they had shed upon the land, and for their idols wherewith they had polluted it: *[19]-*and I scattered them among the heathen, and they were dispersed through the countries: according to their way and according to their doings I judged them"*—**Ezekiel 36:16–19 (KJV)**.

The people of Israel were scattered throughout the world because of their spiritual backsliding, idolatry, and general rebellion against God, as well as their refusal to listen to God's Word presented to them by God's prophets. They have suffered more than any other race of people.

Although this book shows you that your future is bright, I want you to see that drifting away from God and dabbling in sin not only brings great hurt and suffering, it stops the flow of God's blessings into anyone's life.

ELDON'S PROVERBS AND MEMORY VERSES

GOD'S WORD: 1   REAL RICHES

1. You may have nothing in this world, but if you have Jesus and his Word you are rich.

2. Joy forevermore comes from God's Word.

3. The Word of God is a lamp unto my feet, a light into my pathway. When I'm trusting God's Word as my guide, I cannot stumble or fall as I travel life's pathways.

4. Bathe your life in God's Word.

5. Let God's Word heal your broken heart.

6. Proverbs were written to teach God's people how to live and how to act in every circumstance.

7. God wants to mold and shape our lives with his Word.

8. Let God's Word become alive to you.

9. God is in his Word, and I have learned that when I feast upon his Word, I have everything I could ever need in life.

10. Feed on God's Word; let God's Word redeem your life from destruction.

11. Find real living through God's Word.

Eldon Bollinger

As we seek first the kingdom of God and his righteousness, and as we become doers of God's Word, God releases his favor into our lives. Nothing will make your life richer or better than God's favor upon it. For the man of God, God has already released favor into your future. All things work together for your good; the blessings of God will abound in your life, you will see God's favor everywhere you go, and you must believe in and expect it. Ask God every day for His favor upon your life and your family.

Nothing can stop God's favor except you. You may go out and things may look bad, but God will turn things around and cause them to be a blessing for you. You may make bad business decisions, but God will cause it to work out for your benefit, as long as His favor is upon your life.

God already has your life planned out from start to finish, and as long as you stay in faith, the things God has planned will happen. Your future is bright, and only you can prevent good things from happening.

CHAPTER 19

THE WORKING OF THE WORD

[20]*"My son, attend to my words; incline thine ear unto my sayings.* [21]*Let them not depart from thine eyes; keep them in the midst of thine heart.* [22]*For they [my Words] are life unto those that find them, and health to all their flesh"*—**Proverbs 4:20–22 (KJV).**

Eldon's Proverbs and Memory Verses

SUCCESS 1: REAL RICHES

1. In everything you do, put God first, and he will direct you and crown your efforts with success.

2. Real riches are found within.

3. *"There is that which maketh himself rich, yet hath nothing: there is that which maketh himself poor, yet hath great riches"*—**Proverbs 13:7 (ASV).**

4. A man is rich according to what he is, not according to what he has.

5. He who wants milk should not sit on the stool in the middle of the pasture and expect the cow to back up to him.

6. If the task is once begun, never leave it until it is done, either labor great or small–do it well or not at all.

7. Commit your work to the Lord.

8. Failure is usually caused by lack of determination, not lack of talent.

9. The train of failure usually runs on the track of laziness.

10. The secret of success is to start from scratch and to keep on scratching.

11. To be successful, look for work after you have found a job.

12. The reason some people don't recognize opportunity is because it often comes disguised as hard work.

Eldon Bollinger

"It is the spirit that quickeneth; the flesh profiteth nothing: <u>the words that I speak into you, they are spirit and they are life"</u>—**John 6:63 (KJV)**.

"...I commend you to God, and to the Word of his grace, which is able to build you up..."—**Acts 20:32 (KJV).**

God's Word brings life, his abundance, his wisdom, and his health. These all become ours as we live in the Word. Develop a love for God's Word. Hunger and thirst after God's wonderful, vibrant Word. Develop a longing for the Word. Desire the sincere milk of the Word that ye may grow thereby.

Develop a lifelong attitude in believing God's Word. God watches over his Word to perform it. God is in his Word. As you live in his Word, he lives in you.

"If you abide in me, and my Words abide in you, you shall ask what you will, and it shall be done to you"—**John 15:7 (NKJV).**

Success comes by meditating and acting upon the Word of God. *"This book of the law shall not depart out of thy mouth; but thou shall meditate therein day and night, that thou mayest observe to do according to all that is written therein; for then thou shall make thy way prosperous and then thou shall have good success"*—**Joshua 1:8 (KJV).**

ELDON'S PROVERBS AND MEMORY VERSES

SUCCESS 2: REAL RICHES

1. Success is often just an idea away.

2. A man who refuses to admit his mistakes can never be successful.

3. You don't have to lie awake at night to succeed, just stay awake days.

4. Success comes from God.

5. *"He that is slothful in his work is a brother to him that is a great destroyer"*—**Proverbs 18:9 (KJV)**.

6. The single most important ingredient in the formula of success is the knack of getting along with people.

7. The best way to succeed is to follow the advice you give others.

8. Hard work brings prosperity.

9. Success comes in <u>cans</u>, failure in <u>cannots</u>.

10. Develop your business first, before building your house.

11. Whatsoever you do, do it heartily as unto the Lord and not unto man.

12. Wickedness never brings real success. Only the godly have that.

13. Despise God's Word and find yourself in trouble. Honor it and succeed.

Eldon Bollinger

[1]-*"Blessed is the man that walketh not in the Council of the ungodly, nor standeth in the way it of sinners, nor sitteth in the seat of the scornful.* [2]-*But his delight is in the law of the Lord; and in his* [Word] *doeth he meditate day and night.* [3]-*And he shall be like a tree planted by the river of waters, that bringeth forth his fruit in his season; his leaf also shall not wither; <u>and whatsoever he doeth shall prosper"</u>*—**Psalm 1:1–3 (KJV)**.

I've paraphrased **2 Peter 1:3–4 (KJV)** as follows: <u>His divine power hath given unto us all things that pertain until life and Godliness, through the knowledge of Him, through his exceeding great and precious promises.</u>

"And take the helmet of salvation, and the sword of the spirit, which is the Word of God"—**Ephesians 6:17 (KJV)**. God's Word is the sword, which we have to defeat Satan and his demons. All other items of the Christian armor are for defensive reasons.

Unless a Christian possesses a thorough knowledge of God's Word and how to apply it, he has no weapon of attack, no weapon with which he can actually attack Satan and the powers of darkness and put them to flight. *"...I have written unto you, young man, because ye are strong, and the Word of God abides in you, and you have overcome the wicked one"*—**1 John 2:14 (KJV)**. The reason why these young Christian men were strong and able to overcome Satan was that they had the Word of God abiding in them.

ELDON'S PROVERBS AND MEMORY VERSES

SUCCESS 3: REAL RICHES

1. Work hard and become a leader; the lazy never succeed.

2. Wealth gotten from gambling quickly disappears. Wealth gotten from hard work grows.

3. The Lord blesses good men and condemns the wicked.

4. Hard work means prosperity. Only a fool idles away his time.

5. Telling the truth gives a man great satisfaction and hard work returns many blessings to him.

6. A good man is guided by his honesty; the evil man is destroyed by his dishonest.

7. Seek God first.

8. The evil man gets rich for the moment, but the good man's reward lasts forever.

9. Tackle every task that comes along, and if you fear God, you can expect his blessing.

10. Never cheat. Victory comes from God.

11. Riches can disappear fast, and the king's crown doesn't stay in his family forever, so watch your business interests closely.

12. The Lord's blessing is our greatest wealth. All our work adds nothing to it.

Eldon Bollinger

"...Guard my words as your most precious possession"—**Proverbs 7:2 (LB)**.

[47]-*"Whosoever cometh to me, and heareth my sayings, and doeth them, I will show you to whom he is like:* [48]-*he is like a man which builds a house, and digs deep and laid the foundation on a rock: and when the flood arose and when the stream beat vehemently against the house and could not shake it: for it was founded up on a rock* [the Word]*"*—**Luke 6:47–48 (KJV)**.

CHAPTER 20

GOD'S SUCCESS

You have a measure of the God kind of faith! God's Word says you do. You have a measure of the kind of faith that created the world in the beginning. You have a measure of the mountain moving faith.

"Who satisfieth thy mouth with good things…"—**Psalm 103:5 (KJV)**.

"…No good thing will he withhold from them that walk uprightly"—**Psalm 84:11 (KJV)**.

"Blessed be the Lord, which daily loadeth us with benefits…"—**Psalm 68:19 (KJV)**.

"Because thy loving kindness is better than life, my lips shall praise thee"—**Psalm 63:3 (KJV)**.

"The steps of a good man are ordered by the Lord: and he delighteth in his way"—**Psalm 37:23 (KJV)**.

"The young lions do lack, and suffer hunger: but they that seek the Lord shall not want any good thing"—**Psalm 34:10 (KJV)**.

"...Let the Lord be magnified, which hath pleasure in the prosperity of His servant"—**Psalm 35:27 (KJV)**.

[1]"Praise ye the Lord, blessed is the man that feareth the Lord, that delighteth greatly in his commands, [2]his seed shall be mighty upon the earth. [3]Wealth and riches shall be in his house"—**Psalm 112:1–3 (KJV)**.

He shall not be afraid of evil tidings; his heart is fixed trusting in the Lord"—**Psalm 112:7(KJV)**.

"...God has dealt to every man the measure of faith"—**Romans 12:3 (KJV)**.

ELDON'S PROVERBS AND MEMORY VERSES

FAITH 9:   REAL RICHES

1. Stagger not at the promises of God through unbelief.

2. Faith works through the darkness.

3. Because the Lord is my refuge, no evil shall befall me.

4. The righteous flourish like the palm tree.

5. Nothing is secure in life until you learn to trust God.

6. Examine yourself–do you really believe God's Word?

7. Faith sees God at work.

8. Faith sees Satan at work.

9. Faith and works go together.

10. Faith always sees.

11. All unbelief is the belief of a lie.

12. Never put a question mark where God puts a period.

13. I know not what the future holds, but I know who holds the future.

14. If you have faith as a grain of mustard seed, nothing shall be impossible to you.

Eldon Bollinger

"So then faith cometh by hearing, and hearing by the Word of God"—**Romans 10:17 (KJV)**.

Faith for salvation comes when we hear the Word taught! Faith grows and becomes strong as we continue to hear God's Word. <u>Faith is the most important subject in the Bible! You cannot be saved without faith.</u> *"For by grace are ye been saved through faith; and that not of yourself, it is the gift of God"*—**Ephesians 2:8 (ASV)**.

God's gift to you is salvation through faith. *"But without faith it is impossible to please him: for he that cometh to God must believe that he is, and that he is a rewarder of them that diligently seek him"*—**Hebrews 11:6 (KJV)**.

The Christian walk is a walk of faith! <u>"For we walk by faith, not by sight"</u>—**2 Corinthians 5:7 (KJV)**.

ELDON'S PROVERBS AND MEMORY VERSES

FAITH 10:   REAL RICHES

1. Develop your faith until you have no fear of the grave.

2. Faith always sees the rainbow.

3. When fear enters, faith has left.

4. Faith and fear do not mix.

5. Faith allows you to see in the darkness.

6. If you really and fully understand God's love, you will not fear.

7. Don't always try to understand; trust God, and afterward you will understand.

8. God is my refuge and my fortress. In him shall I trust.

9. The righteous shall flourish like the palm tree: he shall grow like the cedars of Lebanon. Those that be planted in the house of the Lord shall flourish in the courts of our God. They shall bring forth fruit in old age. They should be fat and flourish.

10. Because I have set my love upon God, therefore will he deliver me: he will set me on the high because I have known his name.

11. Loving, believing, and trusting brings faith.

Eldon Bollinger

The blind, with their hand in God's, can see more clearly than those who have no faith. Doubt and unbelief are our biggest enemies, and we cannot please God when we allow doubt and unbelief into our lives. 16-"Do not err, my beloved brethren. 17-Every good gift and every perfect gift is from above and cometh down from the Father..."— **James 1:16–17 (KJV).**

12-*"And on the morrow, when they were come from Bethany, he was hungry:* 13-*and seeing a fig tree afar off having leaves, he came, if happily he might find anything thereon: and when he came to it, he found nothing but leaves; for the time of figs was not yet.* [14]*And Jesus answered and said unto it, 'No man eat fruit of thee hereafter forever.' And His disciples heard it"*—**Mark 11:12–14 (KJV).**

[20]*"And in the morning, as they passed by, they saw the fig tree dried up from the roots.* [21]*And Peter calling to remembrance saith unto him, 'Master, behold, the fig tree which thou cursed is withered away'"*—**Mark 11:20–21 (KJV).**

"And Jesus answering saith unto them, 'Have faith in God'" [or have the God kind of faith] —**Mark 11:22 (KJV).**

Mark 11:23 (KJV), *"For verily I say unto you, That whosoever shall say unto this mountain, Be thou removed, and be thou cast into the sea; and shall not doubt in his heart, but shall believe that those things which he saith shall come to pass; he shall have whatsoever he saith."*

"Therefore I say unto you, 'Whatsoever things ye desire, when ye pray, believe that ye receive them, and ye shall have them"—**Mark 11:24 (KJV).**

ELDON'S PROVERBS AND MEMORY VERSES

FAITH 11:   REAL RICHES

1. If you want power with God, feed your spiritual body as often and as much as you feed your physical body!

2. Feed your faith, if you're going to be fat, let it be the hidden man of the heart.

3. God's Word produces faith when acted upon.

4. Don't dig up in doubt what you plant in faith.

5. Faith is like radar—it sees through the fog.

6. Faith is now: it believes now, it acts now, it receives now.

7. Believing God's Word is good, but it does not become faith until you act on it.

8. Your physical body will become sickly, weak, and dried up if it only gets one or two meals a week. Your faith life will become sickly, weak, and dried up if it only gets one or two "meals" a week.

9. Your mind doesn't stay renewed any more than your hair stays combed.

10. I am not moved by what I see. I am not moved by what I feel. I am moved by what I believe.

11. Great victories come from great battles.

Eldon Bollinger

"We having the same spirit of faith, according as it is written, I believed, and therefore have I spoken; we also

believe, and therefore speak"—**2 Corinthians 4:13 (KJV)**.

We have the same spirit of faith that Jesus had when he commanded the fig tree. We're not trying to get it. We're not praying for it. We're not hoping for it, not struggling to get it: we have it now! In the midst of tests and trials, just remember: Jesus is always there. "He hath said, 'I will never leave thee, nor forsake thee"—**Hebrews 13:5 (KJV)**.

"Greater is he that is in you, then he that is in the world [Satan]." The greater one is in you—**1 John 4:4 (KJV)**.

British evangelist Smith Wigglesworth once said, "I am a thousand times bigger on the inside than I am on the outside." He was referring to his faith.

It's up to you what you do with your faith–you can have ever-increasing faith or an exceedingly growing faith. Many Christians feed their bodies three hot meals a day but their spirits one cold snack a week. And they wonder why they're so weak in faith. If you ate one cool snack a week, you would grow weak physically. The same is true spiritually. God's Word is faith food!

Our faith must not be in our feelings. Abraham and God called things that be, not as though they were! *"...blessed are they that have not seen, and yet have believed"*—**John 20:29 (KJV)**.

Faith calls those things that be not as though they were! You will always get your needs met when you believe God's Word and act upon it! <u>God's Word will always work for anyone who dares to believe and act upon it!</u> God wants his people to have abundant provision! *"But my God shall supply all your need according to his riches in glory by Christ Jesus"*—**Philippians 4:19 (KJV).**

You see, this is talking about supplying all your needs, including your financial, material, and other needs. In fact, in this particular chapter in Philippians, Paul is talking about financial and material things because in the previous verse, it says these people had given of their material substance. *"For you know the grace of our Lord Jesus Christ, that, though he was rich, yet for your sakes he became poor, that yea through his poverty ye might be rich"*—**2 Corinthians 8:9 (KJV).**

People misinterpret the word "rich." Someone may say, "You mean God is going to make me a millionaire?" The word rich, according to the dictionary, means a full supply. In other words, it means abundant provision. Isn't that what **Philippians 4:19** says? *"But my God shall supply all your need according to his riches in glory by Christ Jesus."* It didn't say, "But my God shall supply half of your need"–no, it says *all* of them. It promises a full supply!

Jesus said in **Matthew 6:33 (KJV),** *"But seeking ye first the kingdom of God, and his righteousness; and all these things shall be added unto you!"* This Scripture didn't say all these things shall be subtracted from you.

No! These things shall be *added* unto you. Now what are these things? They are material things: something to eat, something to wear, and so on. In other words, the material things in life.

So many people think it is a mark of spirituality to go through life with the soles of their shoes worn out, the seat of their pants worn out, and just barely getting along. But that isn't what Jesus said. He said all these things shall be added unto you, not taken away. I believe **2 Corinthians 9:8 (KJV)** is probably the best definition of success and prosperity ever written, *"And God is able to make all grace abound toward you; that ye, always have all sufficiency in all things, and may abound to every good work."*

It stands to reason that if you have only the bare necessities of life, you are not prosperous and successful. If you have all the necessities of life but no more, that is not prosperity for you are still barely getting by, your cup is not yet running over.

However, if you have everything you need and something left over for the poor that is prosperity. If, after you have paid your tithe on your normal income, you still have something you can give to the missionaries in the field who are preaching the Word of God, who spread the gospel through his Word to those who do not know him that is prosperity.

CHAPTER 21

THE MISSING ELEMENT OF FAITH

<u>I believe being fully persuaded, confident, full of hope, and boldness, are the elements that make up expectation and expectation is the ingredient needed to activate and propel your faith.</u>

"According to my earnest expectation and my hope"—**Philippians 1:20 (KJV).**

"And [Abraham] *being fully persuaded that, what he had promised, he was able to perform"*—**Romans 4:21 (KJV).**

"For the LORD shall be thy confidence, and shall keep thy foot from being taken"—**Proverbs 3:26 (KJV).**

"And now abideth faith, hope, love, these three; but the greatest of these is love"—**1 Corinthians 13:13 (ASV).**

"And now, Lord, behold their threatenings: and grant unto thy servants, that with all boldness they may speak thy Word"—**Acts 4:29 (KJV).**

Although God's Word promises everything that we could ever need or want through his exceeding great and precious promises, many Christians say they seldom see their prayers answered. What is the problem? I believe the struggles of life–the guilt complexes, sin, and the devil have caused them to lose their hope, their confidence, their boldness, and therefore they no longer really expect God to answer their prayers. They hope he will but do not really expect him to.

22-"Let us draw near with a true heart in full assurance of faith, having our hearts sprinkled from an evil conscience, and our bodies washed with pure water. 23- Let us hold fast the profession of our hope without wavering; (for he who promised is faithful that promised)"—**Hebrews 10:22–23 (KJV)**.

We are to live by our faith. Does your prayer always produce the results that you pray for? Does it always produce the results you are confessing and believing for? Are you seeing the manifestation of God's promises in your life? God never intended for his children to beg, bargain, and plead for his promises to be fulfilled in their lives. His great desire is that you receive the full manifestation of every promised blessing. That should include total provision, prosperity, radiant health, well-being, and deliverance from all oppression.

However, that is not what is happening in most Christians' lives in spite of their confessing, believing, and claiming. They are not experiencing that kind of life. The reason is simple. They lack the one key ingredient that would energize their faith and make their prayer life effective, and that ingredient is expecting (hope, confidence, boldness) and being fully persuaded that God would do exactly what he said he would do.

Expectation is the force that launches your faith. It propels faith forward the way rocket boosters propels the space shuttle into orbit. Trying to operate your faith without the force of expectation is like trying to take off in an airplane that has no engine. There's probably nothing wrong with the structure of the plane. It is simply missing a crucial element.

When you're full of expectation, you know God's Word is going to produce exactly what it says it will. And that's not only when the circumstances look good. True confidence is being fully persuaded that no matter what the circumstances look like, God's Word always works.

How do you develop that kind of confidence? That kind of confidence comes through the study of God's Word and allowing the Word to renew a right spirit within you. That wisdom, knowledge, and understanding come from the study of God's Word, and you need a great biblical understanding of what it is and how it works. Remember Abraham was fully persuaded that what God had promised, he was able to perform or would perform.

I believe God wants to answer each and every one of your prayers, especially when they are prayed in line with his Word. However, your prayers must be prayed with faith and expectation. <u>Faith is incomplete without great expectation.</u>

2 Timothy 3:1–7 (KJV)

1 *This know also, that in the last days perilous times shall come.*

2 *For men shall be lovers of their own selves, covetous, boasters, proud, blasphemers, disobedient to parents, unthankful, unholy,*

3 *without natural affection, trucebreakers, false accusers, incontinent, fierce, despisers of those that are good,*

4 *traitors, heady, high minded, lovers of pleasures more than lovers of God;*

5 *having a form of godliness, but denying the power thereof: from such turn away.*

6 *For of this sort are they which creep into houses, and lead captive silly women laden with sins, led away with divers lusts,*

7 *ever learning, and never able to come to the knowledge of the truth.*

Our world is full of religious people. They go to church often, and they do all the religious things, but they deny the power of Almighty God. They don't expect him to move on their behalf. Faith cannot work without the added element of expectation. The force of expectation is what propels your faith and brings the power of God into every situation. <u>Your faith coupled with great expectation will move any mountain and bring victory to every situation.</u>

CHAPTER 22

LIVE AN EXCITING LIFE OF EXPECTATION

Expectation will put your faith into motion and bring victory into everything you do. God knew you before you were born, and he placed goals and dreams within your life that are yet to be developed. It's now time to get excited about your life and to live it in great expectation.

Expectation, confidence, and boldness are the elements that, no matter who you are or what your education is, assure you can have mountain-moving faith with great expectation and confidence. This will always get the results you desire.

Your relationship with Jesus is the key: *"Now when they saw the boldness of Peter and John and perceived that they were unlearned and ignorant man, they marveled; and they took knowledge of them that they had been with Jesus"*—**Acts 4:13 (KJV)**. The disciples in the early church often prayed for boldness they prayed and believed and were filled with boldness.

The force of expecting, coupled with your faith, will move any mountain. *"For verily I say unto you, That whosoever shall say unto this mountain, Be thou removed, and be thou cast into the sea; and shall not doubt in his heart, but shall believe that those things which he saith shall come to pass; he shall have whatsoever he saith"*— **Mark 11:23 (KJV)**.

"According as his divine power hath given unto us all things that pertain unto life and godliness, through the knowledge of him that hath called us to glory and virtue"—**2 Peter 1:3 (KJV)**.

20-*"My son, attend to my words; incline thine ear unto my sayings.* 21-*Let them not depart from thine eyes; keep them in the midst of thine heart.* 22-*For they are life unto those that find them, and health to all their flesh"*— **Proverbs 4:20–22 (KJV)**.

<u>God wants his children to believe everything he has told them in his Word and to expect it to happen just the way he described it.</u> We must demonstrate our faith with expectation, confidence, hope, and boldness with a heart that are fixed, trusting God. Your life will become rich and full with the blessings of God abounding every day, as you learn to incorporate the force of expectation and confidence into your prayer life. All things are possible when you unleash the force of expectation and confidence and join it with your faith.

CHAPTER 23

GOD'S PROTECTION PLAN FOR YOU

LIFETIME WARRANTY

"This know also, that in the last days perilous times shall come"—**2 Timothy 3:1 (KJV)**.

We are truly living in troubling times. The news is full of murders, rape, disasters of every kind, and God's Word says that unless he protects us, guards will do no good.

There can be no doubt, that in these troubling times, the only protection there is, is God and his precious Word! However, the beautiful part of this situation is that God and his Word is all the protection we will ever need! We do not need to fear or live in dread of what may happen when our hearts are fixed, trusting God.

"No weapon that is formed against thee shall prosper; ...this is the heritage of the servants of the Lord"—**Isaiah 54:17 (KJV)**.

"I will say of the Lord, He is my refuge and my fortress..."—**Psalm 91:2 (KJV)**.

"A thousand shall fall at my side, and ten thousand at my right hand; but it shall not come nigh thee"—**Psalm 91:7 (KJV)**.

9-"Because thou hast made the Lord, even the most high, thy habitation; 10-there shall no evil befall thee, neither any plague come nigh thy dwelling, 11-for he shall give his angels charge over thee, to keep thee in all thy ways. 12-They should bear thee up in their hands, lest thou dash thy foot against a stone"—**Psalm 91:9–12 (KJV)**.

"As the mountains are round about Jerusalem, so the Lord is round about his people, from henceforth even forever"—**Psalm 125:2 (KJV)**.

"The angel of the Lord encampeth round about them that fear him, and delivered them"—**Psalm 34:7 (KJV)**.

"Except the Lord build the house, they labor in vain that build it: except the Lord keep the city, the watchmen waketh but in vain"—**Psalm 127:1 (KJV)**.

Our only shield of protection in this troubling time is the shield of faith. The just shall live by their faith. While men's weapons and ways often fail, <u>God's Word never fails and is all the protection we will ever need!</u>

The man of God does not fear or live in dread of what may happen, for he is settled in his mind that Jehovah will take care of him.   This warranty is backed and underwritten by God and his Word.

CHAPTER 24

NEWNESS OF LIFE

"And we know that *all things* work together for good to them that love God, to them who are the called according to *his* purpose"—**Romans 8:28 (KJV)**.

In life there are many struggles: major illnesses, the loss of a job, a broken relationship, the loss of a loved one, and many, many more. We all face major challenges. But God's Word says all things work together for our good. That simply means that no matter what happens and no matter how bad it is, for God's children, when they walk in faith, God will always turn it around and bring something good out of it.

ELDON'S PROVERBS AND MEMORY VERSES

FAITH 12:   REAL RICHES

1. Perfect fellowship with the Lord makes faith as natural as breathing.

2. Exciting words of believing, trusting, and obeying always produce faith.

3. Faith counts the thing done before God has acted.

4. Your words reveal whether your faith is in God's Word or the world system.

5. Your confession shows your faith or your unbelief.

6. Words of doubt and fear destroy faith.

7. Your faith will never rise above your words.

8. Faith and works should travel side-by-side.

9. Your confession propels your faith into action.

10. *"Just as the body is dead when there is no spirit in it, so faith is dead if it is not the kind that results in good deeds"*—**James 2:26 (LB)**.

11. When will you ever learn that believing is useless without doing what God wants you to do? Faith that does not result in good deeds is no real faith at all.

Eldon Bollinger

You are a child of the most high God. You have goals, dreams, and seeds of greatness, and often you leave them on the shelf of life for many years, and they never get planted.

When an animal dies, you bury it in the ground. But, when you prepare your flowerbed, you bury or plant the flower seeds. There's life in the seeds and they come forth and turn into beautiful, fragrant flowers.

Jesus tells us in **John 12:24** that unless a seed or grain of wheat falls into the ground and is planted, it will not produce fruit. Flower seeds or any seed can be stored on the shelf for a lifetime. They will never become what they were created to be until you put them in the ground. Its purpose will never be fully realized until it is planted. Unless it is up on the shelf where it is comfortable, its beauty will never be seen.

We are "planted" when problems and challenges arise. We all face this type of difficulty, but we have the seed of almighty God on the inside of us, and he breathes his life into us. When we go through disappointments or rough times, you may feel as if you've been buried, but the truth is, you have simply been planted. That means you're coming back. You are not only coming back, you're coming back much better and stronger than before.

You go in as a seed, but because of the life of God in you, you come out in newness of life. This newness of life can blossom as a rose, and that seed of greatness that God put in your heart before you were born will suddenly be coming to pass again. What was meant for your harm, God has turned around and made it a blessing for you.

When you plant a fruit seed, one tree comes up, but that tree will produce much fruit, and in each of those fruit are many seeds. We plant a single seed, and it is multiplied many times. That is what this is saying about you. You need to wait with faith and confidence and with a knowing that you are not only coming out of this problem, you will be multiplied and increased and much fruit, or good, will come forth.

What the devil meant for your destruction, God has taken that seed of greatness within you and has multiplied it over and over again. As you stay in faith, it will now wonderfully blossom and bring forth. You can now know that nothing can defeat you, no one can keep you from your destiny. Every problem or set back is only temporary. The Scripture say, let God arise, and his enemies be scattered, and when you let God arise in your life and you show the unshakable confidence in God and his Word, you can expect a great harvest. You can know that your harvest will be better than expected.

Now when difficulties arise and you face new challenges, you don't talk about those difficulties, you can know that your new beginning has arrived. You begin to wonder what great thing God is going to bring out of this, and you anxiously wait. You are now letting God rise in your life and bring forth great things. Yes, now instead of complaining, you say, "I can't wait to see what God will do next."

Trust the Lord who is in you. Learn to become God-inside minded. As you do, God will rise up in you and give illumination to your mind, and he will direct your spirit. You can even look death in the face and laugh because God is in you and you know he is. All things are possible to him who believeth. The Scripture declares that with God, "all things are possible..."—**Mark 9:23 (KJV)**. All things that are possible with God are possible to him who believes because the believer has God, the God with whom all things are possible, dwelling in him.

When others say they don't know what they're going to do, you will say, "I may be in the same situation, naturally speaking, but the greater one is in me! He is in me, and I trust him who dwells in me. He will put me over."

Meditate on truth such as that and feed your spirit on the Word of God. Think on the Holy Spirit's indwelling presence, and see how real the greater one will become to you!

CHAPTER 25

YOU ARE PLANTED, NOT BURIED

When you bury a little seed in the ground, the life in it begins to grow, and one day that little seed breaks the surface of the earth and it grows into a beautiful plant, producing brilliant and colorful flowers. What happened? The seed was planted. It had to go through some dark times, some lonely nights, and had to push tons of dirt out of the way. The seed may have felt that it would never see the bright days again, but it pressed forward. Eventually, it happened just the way God intended–his creation burst through the darkness into the light, grew and flourished.

ELDON'S PROVERBS AND MEMORY VERSES

LOVE 6:   REAL RICHES

1. Is your love patient and kind? Can your love suffer long under the strain of human relations and still be loving and kind? Is your love discouraged by repeated ingratitude and failures on the part of others? And are you nourishing your life with prayer

and Bible study? Is your love of God and the love of the brethren growing and developing? Can you say love and faith and hope are increasing more and more in your life? <u>If so, then your fruit of love and patience are growing and will be a strong force in the healing of others' lives.</u>

2. If God can love me, I sure ought to love others.

3. A home where love abounds <u>is always also abounding in joy, peace, laughter, and happiness.</u>

4. Love is of God, and you cannot hide real love.

5. God is love, and he that dwells in love, dwells in God and God in him.

6. Love grows and develops when given freely.

7. <u>Let love be your greatest aim in life!</u>

8. People who deserve love the least need it the most.

9. As God so loved us, we ought also to love one another.

10. <u>Love cannot be stolen, love cannot be demanded, love can only be given!</u>

Eldon Bollinger

No matter what comes against you in this life, you are not buried, you are planted. It may seem as though you are buried in the dirt because you're going through tough times. It may seem as if your situation will never change, but if you stay in faith and shake off self-pity and negative thoughts, you too, like the little seed, will begin to feel the life of God springing forth within you.

The same power that raised Jesus from the dead is inside you. Just say, "Like the seed, I'm coming back. Things may look bad, but I'm not buried, I'm planted. This is not the end. It's only the beginning."

When you walk by faith, your potential is never buried. Know that whom the Son sets free is free indeed. God has many more victories in your future. Your best is yet to come.

Many times the things we get discouraged about are the very things God uses to promote us. God doesn't allow trials to come into our lives unless he has a purpose and a plan for them. He doesn't send the storms, but he uses them. When you're going through a difficult time, know that this challenge was not sent to destroy you. It was sent to promote and increase you, to strengthen you. Like the little seed you planted, new growth is springing forth in you, new talent, determination, opportunities. God is birthing something in you greater than you are right now. Keep telling yourself, "God is still on the throne. This is not the end. This is only the beginning, I've got comeback power."

Get rid of those feelings of defeat, speak forth in faith, and remember that the only difference between being buried and being planted is what you are expecting and believing for. If you expect this problem to destroy you and your dream, then even though you are a seed with the life of God in you, even though God has already planned your comeback, because of your own disbelieving, it won't happen. If you stay in faith, you will rise above the difficulties to newness of life. You'll see God blossom your life in ways you never imagined. You need to say, "God I know I'm not buried, I'm planted, and I can't wait to see what you will do next for me."

Remember Job? He went through nine months when everything that could go wrong did. He lost his business, his health, his family–everything he had. It looked like God was not concerned about him, and his wife said, "Just curse God and die." Job had been knocked down but was not out. When you read the end of his Bible story, Job came out with twice the blessings he had before. God gave him double for all this trouble.

Instead of complaining, you need to learn to expect God to bring you out much better than when you went in. While you let God rise, you might as well get ready. Your enemies, sickness, death, depression, and disappointment will be scattered; none of those enemies can stay in your way.

Remember, God has planned for you to recover what you've lost and much more. You've been created to overcome every obstacle, to rise above every challenge. I want you to have confidence and assurance that no matter what comes your way, it cannot defeat you. As long as you're letting God rise up within you, your enemies will be scattered.

CHAPTER 26

GOD PLANS FOR YOU TO RECOVER WHAT YOU HAVE LOST

ELDON'S PROVERBS AND MEMORY VERSES

LOVE 8:   REAL RICHES

1. A bit of fragrance always clings to the hand that gives out roses.

2. Through love, serve one another.

3. God is love.

4. Be kind to unkind people; they probably need it the most.

5. Love is warm arms instead of a cold shoulder.

6. Love worketh no ill.

7. Let your love abound.

8. Life is like a mirror: if you frown at it, it frowns; if you smile, it returns the greeting; if you give love, kindness, and happiness, the mirror will return the same to you.

9. <u>Great peace have they who love God's Word.</u>

10. Make your love your way of life.

11. Though I have the gift of prophecy and understand all things, and though I have all faith so that I can move mountains and have not love, <u>I am nothing.</u>

12. By this shall all men know that we are Christians, if we have love one to another.

13. <u>Love is available to everyone.</u>

Eldon Bollinger

Speak forth God's Word, believe that you are a victor and a conqueror, and believe all things work together for good to those who love God, and are called according to his purpose. Believe that no good thing will God withhold from you because, you're a chosen vessel of God.

God told Joshua, "This book of my law shall not depart out of thy mouth, but thou shall meditate therein day and night, that thou mayest observe to do according to all that is written therein for then thou shalt make thy way prosperous and then you shall have good success"—**Joshua 1:8 (KJV).** What God told Joshua applies to us today. He tells us in Deuteronomy 28, if we will observe and do his Word, "…all these blessings shall come on thee and overtake thee…"—**Deuteronomy 28:2 (KJV).**

You are a chosen vessel of God, so expect great things. Believe God for great things, and the river of God's blessing will flow in your life.

CHAPTER 27

HEAVEN AWAITS US

The Scripture says that *Without holiness, no man shall see God: and sin can never enter* [Heaven], see **Hebrews 12:14**.

"He that over cometh shall inherit all things; and I will be his God, and he shall be my son. But the fearful, and unbelieving, and the abominable, and murderers, and whoremongers, and sorcerers, and idolaters, and all liars, shall have their part in the lake which burneth with fire and brimstone: which is the second death"—**Revelation 21:7–8 (KJV)**.

ELDON'S PROVERBS AND MEMORY VERSES

LOVE 9:   REAL RICHES

1. Love makes up for many of our faults.

2. Greater love hath no man than this, that our Lord should lay down his life for us and purchased the forgiveness of our sins.

3. Owe no man anything, but to love one another: for he who loveth another hath fulfilled God's law.

4. The less you open your heart to others, the more your heart suffers.

5. He who dwelleth in love, dwelleth in God.

6. Love plants must be watered with tears and tender care.

7. A friend loveth at all times.

8. Whatever you sow, you shall also reap; let us sow love and we will reap love.

9. Love can bring healing to your life, your family, your world.

10. If God so loved us, we ought also to love one another.

11. <u>Let love rule your life.</u>

12. Choose love as your way of living.

13. The God of love and peace will be with you.

Eldon Bollinger

<u>There is coming a day when the clouds will roll back and Jesus will appear in the clouds to catch his church. I</u>

believe this happens just before the beginning of the great tribulation period, a time of trouble such as the world has never known.

1 Corinthians 15:50–58 (KJV)

50 *Now this I say, brethren, that flesh and blood cannot inherit the kingdom of God; neither doth corruption inherit incorruption.*

51 *Behold, I shew you a mystery; We shall not all sleep [die], but we shall all be changed,*

52 *in a moment, in the twinkling of an eye, at the last trump: for the trumpet shall sound, and the dead shall be raised incorruptible, and we shall be changed.*

53 *For this corruptible must put on incorruption, and this mortal must put on immortality.*

54 *So when this corruptible shall have put on incorruption, and this mortal shall have put on immortality, then shall be brought to pass the saying that is written, Death is swallowed up in victory.*

55 *O death, where is thy sting? O grave, where is thy victory?*

56 *The sting of death is sin; and the strength of sin is the law.*

57 *But thanks be to God, which giveth us the victory through our Lord Jesus Christ.*

58 *Therefore, my beloved brethren, be ye steadfast, unmovable, always abounding in the work of the Lord, forasmuch as ye know that your labor is not in vain in the Lord.''*

1 Thessalonians 4:13–18 (KJV)

13 But I would not have you to be ignorant, brethren, concerning them which are asleep, that ye sorrow not, even as others which have no hope.

14 For if we believe that Jesus died and rose again, even so them also which sleep in Jesus will God bring with him.

15 For this we say unto you by the Word of the Lord, that we which are alive and remain unto the coming of the Lord shall not prevent them which are asleep.

16 For the Lord himself shall descend from heaven with a shout, with the voice of the archangel, and with the trump of God: and the dead in Christ shall rise first:

17 Then we which are alive and remain shall be caught up together with them in the clouds, to meet the Lord in the air: and so shall we ever be with the Lord.

18 Wherefore comfort one another with these words.

We believe the taking away (the Rapture) will take place any day now; signs are everywhere! The Scriptures listed below are signs of the end-time rapture that is to take place, so listen carefully.

10-"Then said he unto them, nation shall rise against nation, and kingdom against kingdom: 11-and great earthquakes shall be in divers places, and famines, and pestilences; and fearful sights and great signs shall there be from heaven"—**Luke 21:10–11 (KJV)**.

25-"And there shall be signs in the sun, and in the moon, and in the stars; and upon the earth distress of nations, with perplexity; the sea and the waves roaring; 26-Men's hearts failing them for fear, and for looking after those things which are coming on the earth: for the powers of heaven shall be shaken. 27-And then shall they see the Son of Man coming in a cloud with power and great glory. 28-And when these things begin to come to pass, then look up, and lift up your heads; for your redemption draweth nigh"—**Luke 21:25–28 (KJV).**

Paul described the end times as perilous times in **2 Timothy 3:1–5 (KJV),** *1-"This know also, that in the last days perilous times shall come. 2-For men shall be lovers of their own selves, covetous, boasters, proud, blasphemers, disobedient to parents, unthankful, unholy, 3-without natural affection, trucebreakers, false accusers, incontinent, fierce, despisers of those that are good, 4-traitors, heady, high-minded, lovers of pleasures more than lovers of God; 5-having a form of godliness, but denying the power thereof: from such turn away."*

I sincerely believe, in light of the prophetic Word, that we are very near to the close of the Gentile church age, and the rapture of the church will soon take place. With this in mind, how important is it to seek the Lord daily, examining our relationship with him, to be sure all is well with our souls and that we are ready every moment of every hour for his soon return?

We must also be about our Father's business, witnessing to lost souls and reaching out to those in need of salvation while there is still opportunity.

Now, let's consider some passage of Scripture that deal directly with the rapture.

1-"Let not your heart be troubled: ye believe in God, believe also in me. 2-In my Father's house are many mansions: if it were not so, I would have told you. I go to prepare a place for you. 3-And if I go and prepare a place for you, I will come again, and receive you unto myself; that where I am, there ye may be also"—**John 14:1–3 (KJV)**.

9-"And when he had spoken these things, while they beheld, he was taken up; and a cloud received him out of their sight. 10-And while they looked steadfastly toward heaven as he went up, behold, two men stood by them in white apparel; 11-which also said, 'Ye men of Galilee, why stand ye gazing up into heaven? This same Jesus, which is taken up from you into heaven, shall so come in like manner as ye have seen him go into heaven'"—**Acts 1:9–11 (KJV)**.

32-"Now learn a parable of the fig tree; When his branch is yet tender, and putteth forth leaves, ye know that summer is nigh: 33-so likewise ye, when ye shall see all these things, know that it is near, even at the doors. 34-Verily I say unto you, this generation shall not pass, till all these things be fulfilled. 35-Heaven and earth shall pass away, but my words shall not pass away. 36-But of that day and hour knoweth no man, no, not the angels of heaven, but my Father only"—**Matthew 24:32–36 (KJV)**.

<u>The questions now arise: Are you ready and are you living a life before God that is acceptable to him? Are you rapture ready?</u>

ELDON'S PROVERBS AND MEMORY VERSES

LOVE 11:   REAL RICHES

1. The measure of a man is not how great his faith is but how great his love is.

2. Those who deserve love the least need it the most.

3. God is love, and we are made in his image.

4. Happiness is the result of circumstances; but joy endures in spite of circumstances.

5. Honor others above yourself.

6. <u>Love heals.</u>

7. Love forgets mistakes.

8. As long as there is love, life is worth living.

9. <u>Love</u> never fails. Love cannot fail.

10. Let us not love in theory or in speech but in truth and in deed.

11. <u>The sweetest joy in life is found in loving and being loved.</u>

12. "And now these three remain: faith, hope, and <u>love</u>, but the greatest of these is love"—**1 Corinthians 13:13 (LB).**

13. Pray for those who spitefully use you.

14. Bless them who curse you.

Eldon Bollinger

CHAPTER 28

OUR CONFESSION

Most Christians have never understood the importance of confession. The Church has never given this important subject much of a place in its teachings and preaching, yet answered prayer, the use of Jesus name and faith are totally and utterly dependent upon it.

"Wherefore, holy brethren, partakers of the heavenly calling, consider the Apostle and High Priest of our profession, Christ Jesus"—**Hebrews 3:1 (KJV).**

"Seeing then that we have a great high priest, that is passed into the heavens, Jesus the Son of God, let us hold fast our confession"—**Hebrews 4:14 (KJV).**

Some translations read profession. But the Greek means witnessing the confession of our lips. [9]-*"That if thou shalt confess with thy mouth the Lord Jesus, and shalt believe in thine heart that God hath raised him from the dead, thou shalt be saved. [10]-For with the heart man believeth unto righteousness; and with the mouth confession is made unto salvation"*—**Romans 10:9–10 (KJV).**

The same place that confession holds in our salvation it also holds in our faith walk. When you confess with your mouth and believe in your heart, you receive salvation. When you confess with your mouth and believe in your heart, you receive your healing, and then we are told to hold fast to our confession.

Christianity is the great confession. We demonstrate our faith by our confession, and we never believe beyond our confession. What we are in Christ and what Christ is to us is demonstrated by our confession. Our confession activates and demonstrates our faith. We will never realize beyond our confession! You will receive from God only that which you confess with your mouth and believe in your heart.

We are to confess God's Word and what the Word says about our situation.

ELDON'S PROVERBS AND MEMORY VERSES

A CHEERFUL HEART 1: REAL RICHES

1. A cheerful and merry heart doeth good like a medicine.

2. <u>A cheerful and merry heart is the result of a heart filled to overflowing with God's peace and love and joy.</u>

3. One can pay a loan back, but you are indebted forever to those who are kind.

4. It takes less time to do a thing right than to explain why you did it wrong.

5. Cheerful and merry hearts produce happy homes.

6. Praise will improve your husband's hearing by at least 50 percent.

7. Children have more need of models than of critics.

8. Real riches are the result of a cheerful and merry heart!

9. Rest in the Lord and wait patiently for him to act.

10. There is no exercise better for the heart than reaching down and lifting someone up.

11. [20]-"Listen, son of mine, to what I say. Listen carefully. [21]-Keep these thoughts ever in your mind. Let them penetrate deep within your heart, [22]-for they [God's Words] mean real life for you and radiant health"—**Proverbs 4:20–22 (LB).**

Eldon Bollinger

[20]- *"My son, attend to my words; incline thine ear unto my sayings. [21]-Let them not depart from thine eyes; keep them in the midst of thine heart. [22]-For they are life unto*

those that find them, and health to all their flesh"— **Proverbs 4:20–22 (KJV).**

We must continually confess what we are in Christ, what he has done for us, what our legal rights are, what the Father has done for us in Christ, what the spirit has done in us through the Word, and what he is able to do through us. We must learn to confess the Word and what it says about us, what we have, and what belongs to us in Christ. <u>Remember, you will never realize beyond your confession!</u>

ELDON'S PROVERBS AND MEMORY VERSES

A CHEERFUL HEART 2:   REAL RICHES

1. <u>A cheerful-hearted person is a real blessing to everyone.</u>

2. A cheerful heart crowds out much unhappiness.

3. Real riches are the riches possessed inside.

4. The love of our Lord and Savior Jesus Christ brings real riches and a cheerful heart to all God's children.

5. Sadness disappears as the cheerful-hearted Christian comes on the scene.

6. God will look you over not for medals, diplomas, or degrees but for scars.

7. Don't worry or fret; it only leads to harm.

8. The Lord's blessing is our greatest wealth.

9. God delights in the prayers of his people.

10. [Neglect] God's Word and find yourself in trouble; obey it and succeed.

11. Guard [God's] words as your most precious possession.

Eldon Bollinger

<u>Make your way of living to have a cheerful heart. It will bring real richness to your spirit and soul and will cause all of those around you to be blessed. Joy and happiness will follow you everywhere you go. Happiness is not a destination but a way of travelling life's roads.</u>

We must be sure we do not have two confessions, one being the confession of God's Word and what we are believing, the other of our doubts and fears and unbelief. We should never confess weakness, failure, doubt, fear, and unbelief because we will always go to the level of our confession, we will go to the level of the words of our mouth.

People often pray sincerely and earnestly, a great prayer of faith in God's Word, and then the next moment they question whether God heard them because they cannot yet see the results. They're not holding fast to their confession of faith, and they are expressing doubt and fear and unbelief. Their last confession destroys their prayer. That kind of praying and believing will never receive anything from God.

Often when we pray for someone's healing and he confesses he is healed, the next words out of his mouth is to ask you to please continue to pray for his healing. With this, he has just destroyed the first prayer.

Our confession must always agree with God's Word, and if you have prayed in Jesus name, you are to hold fast to your confession of faith. It is easy to destroy the effect of your prayer by negative confession.

<u>We must believe before we see the results and we must hold fast to our confession of faith until the results show up.</u>

When I was a teenager at youth camp, I knew a man named Jack Barker. I'll never forget him. He had a large cancer on the right side of his face, and when I ask him about it, he said, "Don't be concerned about it. The Lord <u>has</u> healed it." When I saw him a month later, the cancer was larger and looked very bad. I asked him again about it, and he said the same thing. This went on for many months, and one year later he got out of bed one morning and it was gone. His wife found a big ugly cancer in their bed.

ELDON'S PROVERBS AND MEMORY VERSES

LOVE 12:   REAL RICHES

1. Develop qualities of love, patience, kindness, generosity, humility, unselfishness, forgiveness, and sincerity!

2. Love produces beauty.

3. Love is better than medicine.

4. Live on the high and happy level of love.

5. <u>The love and blessings of God overflows</u> the lives of those who feast upon his Word.

6. We are taught of God to love one another.

7. Love and hate are growing things; cultivate love.

8. Be kindly affectionate to one another.

9. Love is the best, the strongest, and the most rewarding attribute man is capable of cultivating.

10. Love your enemies; be kind to those who hate you.

11. Abide in God's love.

12. He that loveth not knoweth not God, for God is love.

13. *Love one another, for love never fails.*

Eldon Bollinger

"Therefore I say unto you, What things soever ye desire, when ye pray, believe that ye receive them, and ye shall have them"—**Mark 11:24 (KJV)**.

After you pray for whatever your need is, hold fast to your confession of faith, nothing wavering, because you know that what Jesus said will come to pass. So just continue to thank him and praise him for the answer. It cannot fail.

Confession always goes *before* healing and answered prayer. Don't watch symptoms, watch the Word, and be sure your confession is bold and vigorous. Don't listen to people. Act on the Word. Be a doer of the Word. It is God speaking. You are healed. The Word says you are. Don't listen to the senses. Give the Word its proper place in your life. God will not lie, and he watches over his Word to perform it. Remember, all things that pertain to life and godliness have already been given to you through God's exceeding great and precious promises.

ELDON'S PROVERBS AND MEMORY VERSES

A CHEERFUL HEART 3: REAL RICHES

1. He who is of a merry heart hath a continual feast.

2. No good thing will God withhold from those who walk along his path.

3. False friends are like a shadow: they stay around only while the sun shines.

4. Forgiveness is a funny thing. It warms the heart and cools the sting.

5. This is the victory that overcomes the world, even our faith.

6. God's peace and joy is in his Word.

7. Love God's Word more than life, for it will produce real life in you and a cheerful heart.

8. Feasting on God's Word brings real life and radiant health.

9. God's Word is alive and active and will produce your heart's desires.

10. God's Word continues to produce in my life healing and radiant health, life and life more abundantly, joy and peace, richness to my life beyond most minds to comprehend. It is a song in my heart and on my lips that never goes away, a peace that endures and overcomes any trial, a joy the world cannot know and cannot take away. God is in his Word and I have learned that when I trust God's Word, I have

everything I could ever need. I long for the day my Lord returns.

Eldon Bollinger

CHAPTER 29

YOUR FUTURE BEGINS NOW

"Where there is no vision, the people perish..."—
Proverbs 29:18 (KJV).

Many today are so pressed down with the struggles of life, they can't see the future or have goals. Therefore, the condition of their lives will never change. The devil has them whipped.

I continually see people come into the family of God by accepting Jesus Christ as their Lord and Savior, yet they never forsake the ways of the world' they never learn to observe and do God's Word. The great changes God wants to happen in their lives never take place. Those who wish to receive God's blessings and the abundant life God planned for them must forsake the ways of the world and learn to seek first the kingdom of God and his righteousness.

Eldon's Proverbs and Memory Verses

Joy 1:   Real Riches

1. When you have enthusiasm and joy together, your life is the best it can be.

2. Joy produces healing and health.

3. *"These things have I spoken unto you, that my joy might remain in you, and that your joy might be full"*—**John 15:11 (KJV)**.

4. Jesus said that we could have fullness of joy.

5. A joyful heart is of great value.

6. Real joy is a gift from God.

7. Joy in God's creation, so love as he loves.

8. A blanket of gloom destroys our peace, love, joy, and health. The joy of the Lord dispels the gloom!

9. Our lovely daughter (whose name is Joy) calls her mother every morning, and they talk and laugh sometimes for hours. Their laughter rings throughout our home and theirs. I believe it brings health, healing, and great joy to both our homes.

10. Dr. Norman Vincent Peale once said, "You can have peace of mind, improved health, and an ever-

increasing flow of energy. Life can be full of joy and satisfaction."

Eldon Bollinger

CHAPTER 30

HOPE

This lesson is for those who have a great hunger for the things of God, a desire to please God with their lives, and a wish to abound in the blessings of God.

"Return to the stronghold, <u>O prisoners who have no hope</u>; this very day I am declaring that I will restore double to you"—**Zechariah 9:12 (NASB)**.

Zechariah is telling us to be prisoners of hope, to look for and expect God to show up and to shower upon us his abundant favor!

If you are a prisoner of something, you can't get away from it. That's what I want for your life, to continually look for and expect God to move on your behalf. You could become a prisoner of despair, worry, doubt, and discouragement. Don't allow that to happen; become a "prisoner" of hope. Don't allow negative thoughts and words to control your life. Speak forth words of hope and victory. Your thought life and your words will eventually control your life. Make them words of victory.

Blessings abound as you stay in faith. Don't let negative people destroy your optimistic faith. Tell your doubters, "I don't just think it will happen, I know what will happen, and I'm a prisoner of hope. I will not let myself get negative, I will not let myself complain, and hope feeds my faith and lifts my spirit. My best is yet to come! Every day declare that God's promised blessings will come to pass in my life.

We walk by faith and not by sight. We don't have to see to believe, we believe because God said it. We believe and say it first and then we see it.

I believe in praying **Psalm 103:1–5 (KJV)**, [1]"Bless the LORD, O my soul: and all that is within me, *bless* his holy name. [2]Bless the LORD, O my soul, and forget not all his benefits: [3]who forgiveth all thine iniquities; who healeth all thy diseases; [4]who redeemeth thy life from destruction; who crowneth thee with loving kindness and tender mercies; [5]who satisfieth thy mouth with good *things; so that* thy youth is renewed like the eagle's."

God has declared no good things will he withhold from me because I walk uprightly. I believe right now he is arranging things in my favor because I am a prisoner of hope.

I have broken the chains of doubt, fear, worry, self-pity, and negativity because I am a prisoner of hope, and I expect God's favor on everything I do. I believe he is working in and for my life right now.

2- "But his delight is in the law of the LORD; and in his law doth he meditate day and night. 3-And he shall be like a tree planted by the rivers of water, that bringeth forth his fruit in his season; his leaf also shall not wither; and whatsoever he doeth shall prosper. 4-The ungodly are not so: but are like the chaff which the wind driveth away. 5- Therefore the ungodly shall not stand in the judgment, nor sinners in the congregation of the righteous"—**Psalm 1:2–5 (KJV)**.

ELDON'S PROVERBS AND MEMORY VERSES

JOY 2:   REAL RICHES

1. The Lord is the joy of my life.

2. The joy of the Lord is my strength.

3. When wisdom and truth enter the very center of your being, they fill your life with joy.

4. Rejoice in the Lord always, and again I say rejoice.

5. Joy and enthusiasm are partners, and they bring great happiness.

6. One way to joy is laughter.

7. Live the joyful way.

8. The person with the peace and joy of God in his heart is always successful, no matter what problems he faces in this life.

9. Rejoice and be exceedingly glad because your joy comes from the Lord and the joy of the Lord is your strength.

10. Joyfully love the world and its beauty and its people.

Eldon Bollinger

No matter the problems you face today, hold onto your faith. **Hebrews 10:35** tells us to <u>not cast away our confidence, for it will be richly rewarded.</u> That is telling us to stay in faith, for if we keep believing, keep hoping, keep doing the right thing, God promises there will be a rich reward. If you will keep believing, keep hoping, keep doing the right thing, and if you stay in faith and stay strong for the final push, you will see the situation turn around. You will see the promised blessings come to pass.

Your future begins now, as you learn to do things God's way and according to his Word. His favor is instantly upon your life, and with God, all things are possible. God is in complete control, and you're a prisoner of hope, so get up each day and expect God's favor. Not only that, but you are one of God's children, and he prides himself on the care and love he gives his children. Remember, he said no good things will I withhold from my children or from those who walk uprightly.

ELDON'S PROVERBS AND MEMORY VERSES

JOY 3: REAL RICHES

1. In a world of much heartache, the man of God can rest in God's peace and love and joy.

2. God will fill your life with laughter and your lips with great joy.

3. Bring a sacrifice of joy into the house of the Lord.

4. A joyful Spirit is a great blessing to everyone.

5. Rejoice with exceedingly great joy.

6. Demonstrate to everyone the joy of the Lord.

7. You shall go out with joy and be led forth with peace.

8. Let God fill your life with pure joy.

9. A spoonful of joy is better than a spoonful of medicine.

10. Sing for joy, O heavens, shout the whole earth, bring forth with songs old mountains.

11. Therefore the redeemed of the Lord shall return and come with singing unto Zion: and everlasting joy shall be upon their heads.

Eldon Bollinger

Did you know God's favor is for a lifetime? As long as you stay in faith and please God with your life, his favor will follow you all the days of your life. There is no want for the children of God who walk uprightly and please God with their lives, because God's favor is upon their lives, and he blesses everything they do. He tells us in **Romans 8:28 (KJV)**, *"All things work together for good to them that love God and are called according to his purpose."* Did you understand that? *All* things. Not *some* things, but all things will work for my good when I please God with my life.

CHAPTER 31

LOST OPPORTUNITIES RECOVERED

God is a God of love and mercy. His kindness goes on and on forever. There is nothing he won't do for his children who obey him and walk with him. He forgives our sins, heals our bodies, redeems our life from destruction, and crowns us with loving kindness and tender mercy.

However, he is also a God of judgment, and those who go their own way and forsake their God bring disaster upon their lives. That is what happened many times to the children of Israel. But, God is a God of great mercy and forgiveness, and when you ask him for forgiveness and turn to him with all your heart, he will forgive your sins and will establish you as a holy person. <u>And the opportunities you have lost he will recover for you.</u> When you believe in the Lord Jesus Christ and ask him to forgive your sins, he immediately does that and cleanses you from all unrighteousness. You are redeemed from Satan's dominion, and when you put on the righteousness of God in Christ, it is as if you had never sinned.

From the book of Malachi, we read about a time when the children of Israel drifted away from God, went their own ways, and got heavily involved in sin and everything except obeying and worshiping God. They went to church, they did the religious things, but they did not obey and do God's Word. God's blessings stopped, and disaster struck their lives. Then they cried unto the Lord and said, "Why are you not blessing us?"

In **Malachi 3:7–11 (KJV)** God replies, [7]-*"Even from the days of your fathers ye are gone away from mine ordinances, and have not kept them. Return unto me, and I will return unto you, saith the LORD of hosts. But ye said, wherein shall we return?* [8]-*Will a man rob God? Yet ye have robbed me. But ye say, wherein have we robbed thee? In tithes and offerings.* [9]-*Ye are cursed with a curse: for ye have robbed me, even this whole nation.* [10]-*Bring ye all the tithes into the storehouse, that there may be meat in mine house, and prove me now herewith, saith the LORD of hosts, if I will not open you the windows of heaven, and pour you out a blessing, that there shall not be room enough to receive it.* [11]-*And I will rebuke the devourer for your sakes, and he shall not destroy the fruits of your ground; neither shall your vine cast her fruit before the time in the field, saith the LORD of hosts."*

[24]-*"Therefore whosoever heareth these sayings of mine, and doeth them, I will liken him unto a wise man, which built his house upon a rock:* [25]-*and the rain descended, and the floods came, and the winds blew, and beat upon that house; and it fell not: for it was founded upon a rock.*

26 *And every one that heareth these sayings of mine, <u>and doeth them not</u>, shall be likened unto a foolish man, which built his house upon the sand:* **27** *and the rain descended, and the floods came, and the winds blew, and beat upon that house; <u>and it fell: and great was the fall of it</u>"—* **Matthew 7:24–27 (KJV).**

We see from all of this that many who never knew the Lord and many who once knew the Lord, drifted away, and returned to the ways of sin and Satan cannot expect to receive the river of blessings that God offers his children who obey him.

ELDON'S PROVERBS AND MEMORY VERSES

JOY 4:   REAL RICHES

1. The counselor of peace is joy. In thy presence is fullness of joy.

2. They who sow in tears shall reap in joy.

3. The meek shall increase in the joy of the Lord.

4. Rejoice with joy all you who morn.

5. These things have I spoken unto you, that my joy might remain in you and your joy might be full.

6. For you shall go out with joy and be led forth with peace: the mountains and hills shall break forth

before you into singing, and all the trees in the field shall clap their hands. Instead of the thorn shall come up the fur tree and instead of this briar shall come up the myrtle tree, and [joy] shall be to the Lord for a name, for an everlasting sign that shall not be cut off, praise God.

7. He who is of a merry heart hath a continual feast.

8. Sorrow and mourning shall flee when gladness and joy arrive.

9. Make your words good words, joyful words.

10. A man has joy by the words of his mouth.

Eldon Bollinger

CHAPTER 32

RECOVER WHAT YOU HAVE LOST

The storms of life may come. At times, it might look like you're finished, that it's all over for you. If you're one of these people, God wants to welcome you back and for you to recover that which you have lost, to redeem your life from destruction, and to pour out his love and blessings upon your life once again.

If, on the other hand, you are a dedicated Christian, in fellowship with God, and the cares and struggles of life have just almost defeated you and kept you whipped down, that's the work of Satan trying to destroy you.

You may not know what belongs to you as a member of the family of God, and you may not have learned how to walk by faith or to receive the fullness of God's love and blessings. You may not be believing in and expecting the great things God has planned for your life. The enemy, or Satan, may have done his best, but his best will never be enough. If you stay in faith, what was meant to stop you will not be a stumbling block but a stepping-stone, taking you to a higher level. Keep your hopes high, and expect and believe in God for great things.

You are not average. You are not ordinary. You are a child of the Most High God. Life may have dealt you a tough blow. At times, it may feel like the wind has been let out of your sails. However, the good news is Almighty God has put a recovery program in your spirit. You can bounce right back and recover what has been stolen from you. God has promised that what was meant to harm you, he will use for your good.

When you become a bounce-back person, you will know that every adversity, every setback is only temporary that will not last forever. Weeping may endure for the night, but you know joy is coming in the morning. So don't sit around complaining, thinking about how bad it was and everything you've lost. God is a God of restoration. He has promised to pay you back double for every unfair situation. Instead of becoming discouraged by the difficulty, you're encouraged by challenges because you know you will receive double for your trouble! Yes, in spite of your challenges today tomorrow will come out better than it was before. Keep your hopes high!

God holds you in the palm of his hand. He knows every struggle, every lonely night, and every unfair situation. A little sparrow cannot fall to the ground without God knowing about it. How much more is God concerned about you and me, his sons and daughters? The Scriptures say, *"...When the enemy comes in like a flood..."*—**Isaiah 59:19 (KJV)**. That means when you feel overwhelmed when the hurricane hits or the stock market drops, what does God do? He doesn't say, "Too bad. I told you life was hard. You should have made better decisions." No. When the enemy comes in like a flood, God raises up a barrier. In other words, it gets God's attention. He does not sit back and make us fight our battles on our own. That's when he steps up to turn things around in our favor.

CHAPTER 33

YOUR DAY OF VICTORY IS COMING 1

When they crucified Jesus, it was a dark day, probably the most painfully discouraging day of his life. In fact, it was so bad, Jesus earlier sweat great drops of blood. It probably looked like his life was over. Most people thought his enemies had finished him. But, God had other plans. Although they put his body in a grave, three days later, he arose victorious.

Death could not keep him in the grave. The forces of darkness could not stop him. On the third day, Jesus came out of the grave and said, *"...I was dead, and behold, I am alive for evermore..."*—**Revelation 1:18 (ASV)**. No matter how dark it looks, no matter how long it has been, no matter how many people are trying to push us down, if we stay in faith, God will turn things around for us.

You may have problems in your path. You can't see how you can never accomplish your dreams, or how you can recover your health, or resolve your problems. Negative thoughts are bombarding you: it may seem to be all over, that it will never be any better. However, God has the final say! God's Word declares that all things work together for good to those who love God and are called according to his purpose. <u>God has the final say, and your day of victory is coming.</u>

When God put those dreams in your heart, he made plans to see them fulfilled. The good news is he already has a completion date for them. You may not see how that could happen. It may be taking a long time. The odds appear to be against you. However, if you just keep believing, keep praying, keep being your best, God will cause those dreams to become a reality. <u>Your day of victory is on its way.</u>

Although problems might look overwhelming, God is not limited by things. He's got resurrection power; he can give you one break that will put you on a new level of life. He can open doors that no man can shut. He can bring talent out of you that you didn't know you had. He can send people who will go out of their way to be good to you.

ELDON'S PROVERBS AND MEMORY VERSES

JOY 5:   REAL RICHES

1. **Ecclesiastes 9:9 (JB)** says, *"Live happily with the woman you love, through the fleeting days of life. For the wife God gives you is your best reward down here for all your earthly toil and I can honestly say that my wife, who the Lord gave me is my greatest*

joy here on the earth, and my children are the source of much joy."

2. All things that pertain to life and godliness are ours through God's Word, so enjoy, enjoy, enjoy.

3. Let the joy bells ring; enjoy God's peace.

4. Lord, we have great joy in thy loving kindness.

5. Everyday declare the joy of the Lord as your strength.

6. Oh what joy for those whose sins are forgiven!

7. Joy comes in the morning–shout for joy.

8. Joy drives out sadness; when you are filled with God's Spirit, joy will always follow.

9. When joy is within, it will always show on your face.

10. Enjoy God's loving kindness.

Eldon Bollinger

Just keep believing and praying and you will come into your supernatural increase. When your path seems darkest you feel lost and defeated, so make a declaration of faith and declare, "I know my day of victory is almost here!" What you're really saying is, "God, I know you will turn this situation around, and I know you will heal my body or meet whatever need I have."

Don't be discouraged and complain; speak to the problem and speak victory over your circumstances. **Philippians 1:6 (NLT)** states that <u>God will bring you to a flourishing finish</u>, so God will finish what he started with you, and it will turn out bigger and better than you ever imagined. Just stay in faith and be the person you know God wants you to be. Whatever your dream, the good news is, God already has a completion date for you.

When you are tempted to get discouraged, just turn it around, say, "Father, I want to thank you that you finish what you started in my life. I know you are God of completion."

Remember, it's not by our own might or power that our lives are completed. We reach fulfillment when God releases his favor into our dreams, so hold fast to what God put in your heart. Stay determined and go out each day in faith and expectancy.

ELDON'S PROVERBS AND MEMORY VERSES

JOY 6:   REAL RICHES

1. <u>You have a choice:</u> you can choose to be happy, with joy, or you can let the cares of this life and the problems you face make you unhappy, bitter,

resentful, and critical–and Satan will have you defeated.

2. Choose God's way: let the joy of the Lord be your strength.

3. So, shall my Word be that goeth forth out of my mouth: it shall not return me void, but it shall accomplish that which I please and shall prosper in the thing where to I send it. Let the joy of the Lord rule your life and his blessings will always follow.

4. Joy is the best therapy there is.

5. Every morning declare the joy of the Lord is my strength.

6. Happiness is the result of circumstances, but joy endures in spite of circumstances.

7. The earth breaks forth in praise to God and sings for utter joy.

8. In thy presence is joy and at the right hand there are pleasures forevermore.

9. A joyful person brings happiness to everyone around him. <u>Be that person</u>.

Eldon Bollinger

CHAPTER 34

SEEDS OF GREATNESS

You may have a future filled with hope, faith, blessing, and promotion. If you are impatient, you may become discouraged. You may feel frustrated, maybe even tempted to make bad decisions, but let me remind you who you are and what you have on the inside. You are a child of the Most High God. You have seeds of greatness inside you. You have royal blood flowing through your veins. You have been crowned with glory and honor. You are destined to leave your mark on this generation. It may not have happened yet, but the promise is still in you. Don't give up on your future. Don't make decisions that you will regret. Let me assure you that great days lie ahead. You will see your dreams come to pass. When it's time for God to promote you, to vindicate you, to restore you, all the forces of darkness cannot stop good things from happening.

You may feel frustrated now, but God is working behind the scene in your life and is arranging the right breaks, the right people, and the right opportunities. Sometimes the process takes longer before all of the pieces are in place. Patience is critical. **Psalm 106** warns that the people of Israel did not wait for God's plan to unfold. They missed their promised land because they became discouraged. They complained and gave up hope. Don't let this happen to you. Stay in faith. Recognize that God may be testing you. If you let his plan unfold, you'll find that God will give you something better than you dreamed.

When is God's appointed time? God knows when the time is correct. When you understand this principle, it takes the pressure off. It's a stress-free way to live, knowing that as long as we stay in faith, God will release his favor, his restoration, his healing at exactly the right time in our lives. Just stay in faith knowing that God will bring your promise to pass, and he will bring it to a flourishing finish! It's time for your restoration. Your best is yet to come!

"For if by one man's offence death reigned by one; much more they which receive abundance of grace and of the gift of righteousness <u>shall reign in life by one, Jesus Christ"</u>—**Romans 5:17 (KJV)**.

<u>Do you reign your life?</u>

ELDON'S PROVERBS AND MEMORY VERSES

FRIENDSHIP 1:   REAL RICHES

1. A friend will strengthen you with his prayers, bless you with his love, and encourage you with his hope.

2. Friendship doubles our joys and divides our sorrows.

3. Pick your friends, but not to pieces.

4. One reason a dog has so many friends: he wags his tail instead of his tongue.

5. A friend loveth at all times.

6. You will gather many friends, if you are truly a friend.

7. Let Jesus be your friend.

8. Gossip separates the best of friends.

9. If you fall down, your friend can help you up. But pity the man who has no friend.

10. The strength of your friendship is determined by what you are willing to give to the friendship.

11. Flattery is insincere friendship.

Eldon Bollinger

Yes, if you want God to fight your battle for you, look up, lift up your head, and get a vision of yourself getting stronger. Your life will follow your vision, so look up. If you lift up your head, the Lord, mighty in battle, will help you. When God shows up, every enemy, every obstacle, every battle will be turned into a victory. When you're observing and doing God's Word and you are in faith, there may be times of great stress, but like the palm tree, you will bounce right back.

Begin today to expect great things, look to God who is the author and finisher of your faith, and you will begin to bounce back from every sickness, from bad relationship problems. You will bounce back from financial difficulties. You will bounce back from a bad attitude. Your setbacks are simply preparing you for a great comeback. You may be a little bent right now, but it's only a matter of time before you come back stronger, increased, healthier, promoted, better off than you were before, and abounding in the blessings of God.

Like Joshua, whatever you do will prosper because you have pleased God with your life and because his favor is upon your life.

ELDON'S PROVERBS AND MEMORY VERSES

FRIENDSHIP 2:   REAL RICHES

1. Real friends may move away. But the friendship always remains.

2. Wealth makes many friends, but when the money runs out, so do the friends.

3. A friend of the world is the enemy of God. **James 4:4 (KJV)**, "Whosoever therefore will be a friend of the world is the enemy of God."

4. People don't care how much you know until they know how much you care.

5. "Let nothing be done through strife or vainglory but in lowliness of mind, and let each esteem others better than themselves" —**Philippians 2:3 (KJV).**

6.

7. A real friend is like Jesus; he will never forsake you.

8. Friends are like a flower garden: the more you care for them, the more they flourish.

9. Choose your friends carefully, for you are known by the friends you keep.

10. The only way to have a friend is to be one.

11. Every person should have a special cemetery plot in which he buries the faults of his friends.

Eldon Bollinger

CHAPTER 35

OUR UNION WITH CHRIST

This teaching has been neglected. I often wonder why a large percentage of those who accept Christ and join the church continue to walk in failure. There is great success in God's Word. I have a study that I teach and I call it success through the Scripture. Although there is great success and victory through the Word of God, a large number of Christians never attain the success Jesus desired. Our victory and success comes through our union with Christ in the new creation, and our communion with him is based on fellowship and relationship.

John 10:10 (KJV) says, "I am come that ye might have life and have it in abundance." What was this life? It was the nature of God. Who was to have it? The man for whom Christ died. **John 3:16 (KJV)** says, "For God so loved the world, that he gave his only begotten Son, that whosoever believeth on him should not perish, but have eternal life."

However, the question is, how are we going to get that eternal life? Jesus illustrated it in his talk with Nicodemus in **John 3.** Jesus said, *"...Except a man be born from* *above, he cannot enter the Kingdom of God"*—**John 3:3 (KJV).**

In addition, **John 3:6–7 (KJV),** [6] *"That which is born of flesh is flesh; and he that is born of the Spirit is spirit.* [7] *Marvel not that I said unto thee, Ye must be born again."*

Now, if we haven't read Paul's revelation, we don't understand that, for we have nothing in Jesus' teaching that explains the nature of the new birth. Jesus merely tells us he is bringing us eternal life and that <u>we must be born again.</u>

ELDON'S PROVERBS AND MEMORY VERSES

WISDOM 7: REAL RICHES

1. If any of you lack wisdom, let him ask of God that giveth to all men liberally and it shall be given unto him.

2. By wisdom, the Lord laid the foundations of the earth.

3. If you add a little to a little and do it often, soon that little becomes great.

4. Real wisdom is correcting your faults.

5. *Wisdom* is a tree of life.

6. Minds are like parachutes: they work best when they are open.

7. Prudently, cautious self-control is wisdom's roots.

8. A wise man has great power, and a man of knowledge increases in strength.

9. <u>How does a man become wise? The first step is to trust and revere the Lord.</u>

10. Knowledge comes and goes, but wisdom lingers.

11. <u>Every young man who listens to me, and obeys my instructions, will be given wisdom and good sense. Yes, if you want better insight and discernment and are searching for them as you would for lost money or hidden treasures, then wisdom will be given unto you, and knowledge of God himself; He will soon learn the importance of reverence for the Lord and trusting in him.</u>

Eldon Bollinger

[17-]*"Wherefore if any man is in Christ, he is a new creature* [creation]*: the old things* [sin, spiritual death, and of union with Satan] *are passed away; behold, all things are become new;* [18-]*But all these things are of God, who reconciled us to himself through Christ"*—**2 Corinthians 5:17–18 (ASV)**.

That is tremendous! The Father has reconciled us unto himself. The things that stood between the Father and us have been eliminated. A new creation has come into existence. The old nature is driven out, and we are new creations in the spirit, just as Adam was a physical new creation in the garden. The spiritual new creation has come into being, imparted to us eternal life that Jesus said he was bringing to the world.

[23]-*"And that ye be renewed in the spirit of your mind,* [24]-*and put on the new man, that after God hath been created in righteousness and holiness of truth"*—**Ephesians 4:23–24 (ASV).**

The new creation is the product of God himself. He, through the spirit, has given birth to a new nature in us.

<u>The old nature of failure, of sin consciousness that was ruled by the adversary and was a part of the adversary, has stopped being. A new nature has taken its place. We are now the very sons and daughters of God Almighty. **Romans 8:14–16 (NKJV)** is a reality, [14]-"For as many as are led by the spirit of God, these are the sons of God. [15]-For you receive not the spirit of bondage again unto fear; but ye receive the spirit of adoption, whereby we cry, Abba, Father. [16]-The spirit Himself bears witness with our spirit, that we are children of God."</u>

ELDON'S PROVERBS AND MEMORY VERSES

WISDOM 8: REAL RICHES

1. Lord, help me fill my thoughts with your words and live so close to you that your wisdom will be my constant companion and a great part of my life.

2. Exalt wisdom and she will promote you.

3. Love wisdom and she will guard you.

4. An enterprise is built by wise planning.

5. Wisdom will place a beautiful crown upon your head.

6. Listen to wisdom and do as she says, and you will have a long and good life.

7. Determination to be wise is the first step toward becoming wise.

8. Lord, give me the wisdom to make stepping-stones out of stumbling blocks.

9. I would have you learn this great fact: a life of doing right is the wisest life.

10. A wise man begins cutting his wisdom teeth the first time he bites off more than he can chew.

11. <u>In everything you do, put God first and he will direct you and crown your efforts with success.</u>

12. The wise are promoted to honor.

Eldon Bollinger

CHAPTER 36

A NEW CREATION

"For the showing, I say, of His righteousness at this present season: that he might himself be just [righteous] *and the justifier* [righteousness] *of him that believeth in Jesus"*—**Romans 3:26 (ASV)**.

You see, you haven't only become a son, but a son with a standing with the Father that he gives you himself. That is perfectly natural that if the Father has sons, he will give them a standing with himself so that they can approach him with the uttermost freedom and liberty. He becomes their righteousness.

You know righteousness means the ability to stand in the Father's presence without the sense of guilt or inferiority, to stand in the presence of Satan without any inferiority, and to stand in the presence of anything Satan has done without any sense of inferiority. You stand in his presence as his master. You are taking Jesus' place in the world, and you are Satan's master because you do it. Now you can have righteousness; you can have eternal life. You can have the consciousness of sonship. You can have the great, mighty Spirit come and make his home in your body because that is the ultimate of the new creation. You see, you are recreated so that your body might become the home of God.

You remember **1 Corinthians 6:19–20 (KJV)**, [19]*"Know ye not that your body is a temple of the Holy Spirit which is in you, which ye have from God, and ye are not your own?* [20]*For ye were bought with a price: therefore glorify God in your body..."*

All this may be true, but you may never have learned the secret of joy. <u>You ask, "What do you mean by joy?"</u> <u>**John 15:10 (KJV)** says, [10]"If ye keep my commandments, ye shall abide in my love; even as I have my Father's commandments and abide in his love." Then we see in the ninth verse another secret: "Even as the Father hath loved me, I also have loved you: abide ye in my love"—**John 15:9 (KJV)**. We are to walk and live in love and to keep His commandments. **John 13:34–35** shows us that the law of the new creation, the law that governs the new creation, is the love law. We are to love one another even as he loved us.</u>

Jesus said, [10]"...Even as I have kept my Father's commandments and abide in his love. [11]These things have I spoken unto you, that my joy may be in you, and that your joy may be made full"—**John 15:10–11 (KJV)**. For years that did not mean anything to my spirit, until one day I saw that the secret of Christianity, the secret of evangelism, was that we were to have joy in our spirits. **1 Peter 1:8 (KJV)** tells us that it is "...joy unspeakable and full of glory." That didn't mean much to me until the spirit unveiled it to me. Then I saw the secret of this new thing was to come with the new creation.

My joy I give unto you. This is something the world cannot take away from me. It is something indescribable that fills our spirits. What does joy grow out of? What is the secret?

"God is faithful, through whom ye were called <u>into the fellowship</u> of his Son, Jesus Christ our Lord"—**1 Corinthians 1:9 (KJV)**. Fellowship is the secret; it is the thing that gives joy. When the fellowship is broken, the joy dies. The happiness of marriage is the fellowship between those two hearts. Misery comes full tide when the fellowship is broken. You may be a child of God and have all the knowledge and the riches that belong to that marvelous relationship, but if you have no fellowship with the Father, there is no joy in your life. It is an empty, dry thing. The power of our ministry lies in our fellowship.
3-*"That which we have seen and heard declare we unto you also, that ye also may have fellowship with us.* [Why?] *And our fellowship is with the Father, and with his Son, Jesus Christ:* 4-*And these things we write, that our joy may be made full"*—**1 John 1:3–4 (ASV)**.

ELDON'S PROVERBS AND MEMORY VERSES

WISDOM 1: REAL RICHES

1. Wisdom is the principle thing; therefore, get wisdom.

2. The fear of the Lord is the beginning of wisdom.

3. He layeth up sound wisdom for the righteous.

4. Wisdom is too high for a fool.

5. A wise man feareth and delivereth from evil.

6. Whoso findeth wisdom findeth life and shall obtain favor of the Lord.

7. Seek wisdom.

8. Happy is everyone who retaineth wisdom.

9. She [Wisdom] is a tree of life to those who lay hold upon her.

10. After winning an argument with your wife, the wisest thing for you to do is apologize.

11. Being unwanted, unloved, uncared for, and forgotten is much worse than having nothing to eat and poverty.

12. The art of being wise is the art of overlooking others' faults.

13. Be tolerant of those who disagree with you. After all, they have a right to their own ridiculous opinions.

14. Wisdom is more precious than rubies.

Eldon Bollinger

There it is. Now what is that fellowship? It is that sweet communion between your spirit and the Father. It is that glad richness that comes through the unveiling of the Word to your spirit.

It is the quiet assurance that fills your heart with an unspeakable, irresistible joy. Faith cannot grow without rich fellowship with the Father. I don't care how much knowledge one has of the Word, if his fellowship is broken, his faith is crippled. The adversary takes advantage of him and holds him in bondage.

CHAPTER 37

WALKING IN DARKNESS

Most people who have chronic physical trouble have an unsatisfactory fellowship with the Father and with the Word. They begin to challenge the faithfulness and the love of God. They say, "Well, if God loves me, why has he afflicted me like this?" You understand the Father has not afflicted them. The adversary has afflicted them, and they have submitted to the adversary's affliction and have lived in misery and bondage. If they had known what held them, they would turn to **1 John 1:5–6 (ASV)** which says, [5]-*"And this is the message which we have heard from him and announced unto you, that God is light, and in him is no darkness at all."* [6]-*If we say we have fellowship with him yet walk in darkness, we do not tell the truth."*

Notice now that if we say we have fellowship and don't know his will, it is evident that we are in darkness. **1 John 2:10–11 (ASV)** tells us, [10]-*"He that loveth his brother abides in light, and there is no occasion of stumbling in him.* [11]-*But he that hateth his brother is in darkness, and walketh in the darkness and knoweth not* *whether he goeth, because the darkness hath blinded his eyes.''* That darkness may come from a hundred reasons.

ELDON'S PROVERBS AND MEMORY VERSES

HAPPINESS 2:   REAL RICHES

1. Happiness is love of your work.

2. The best are not only the happiest, but usually the happiest are the best.

3. Happiness is a clear conscience.

4. God is concerned about your happiness.

5. Joyfulness will prolong your days.

6. Happy is the generous man, the one who feeds the poor.

7. Appreciate the wonders of nature.

8. Happiness brings healing and health.

9. People with time for others are happy around the clock.

10. <u>Count your blessings, not your problems.</u>

11. Joy is everywhere.

12. Happiness is a running stream, not a stagnant pond.

13. Despondency, fear, and discouragement bring sickness and poverty.

14. You can be as happy as you make up your mind to be.

15. Sing, O heaven! Be joyful, O Earth!

Eldon Bollinger

One may have failed in his finances. He hasn't given the Lord his share of his income. He may have failed in speaking to men and women about their souls. It can come from a million different sources. Fellowship can be broken because I willfully fail to do his will. I stepped out of light into the darkness. I stopped practicing love; and when I do that, I step over into darkness, back into Satan's territory. I am filled with restlessness. <u>Joy is gone. My fellowship with the Father is gone. If I say I have fellowship with him and walk in darkness, I lie and do not tell the truth.</u>

<u>When we break fellowship with the Father by refusing to do his will and step out of love, we walk in darkness.</u> No one ever criticizes another believer as long as he is walking in fellowship. All bitterness, criticism, and unkindness are the product of broken fellowship. If we walk in the light, as he is the light, we have fellowship with one another; but if we walk in darkness, we have no fellowship with one another. We have no knowledge of

his will. And the blood of Jesus Christ cleanses us from all sin. That is effective as long as we are in fellowship.

The correct meaning of the Word sin is "missing the mark." As long as I am in fellowship with him, I may miss the mark again and again, but his blood avails for me. Then I deliberately refuse to do his will, and darkness overwhelms me. If I deny that I sinned, I deceive myself, and the reality or truth is not in me. How true that is! The truth is not in me. There is no sense of reality. The Word is no longer a thing of comfort and inspiration.

However, he says if we confess our sins, he is faithful and righteous to forgive us our sins, and to cleanse us from all of the righteousness. In other words, if we say we have not sinned yet are out of fellowship, we do not have the reality of the life in us. **1 John 1:9 (KJV)**, *"If we confess our sins, he is faithful and just to forgive us our sins* [or the thing that stands in the way]. *"* Now we go to **1 John 2:1 (ASV)**, *"My little children, these things I write unto you that you may not sin. And if any man sin, we have an advocate with the Father, Jesus Christ the righteous."*

CHAPTER 38

BROKEN FELLOWSHIP RESTORED

I think this is one of the most marvelous statements in the whole of the epistles [**1 John 2:1**]. Seated at the Father's right hand is our <u>righteous advocate</u>; and the moment that I break fellowship, he is there in fellowship with the Father. I lose my sense of righteousness. He is the righteous one. He is there, in the presence of the Father, to plead my case.

<u>I look up to the Father and say, "Father, forgive me for doing that thing." And the moment I do, he forgives me. It is wiped out as though it had never been. The instant that I confess it and tell the Father of it, Jesus says, lay that to my account. Notice that the Father has no memory of your past mistakes and failures. You must forget them too. "The grace of the Lord Jesus Christ, and the love of God, and the communion of the Holy Spirit, be with you all"—**2 Corinthians 13:14 (KJV)**.</u>

ELDON'S PROVERBS AND MEMORY VERSES

HAPPINESS 3:   REAL RICHES

1. Thank God for the precious gift of life.

2. Reading is inexpensive entertainment that often produces lasting pleasure.

3. Sing with gladness.

4. Banish sadness.

5. Happiness does not come from possessions but from our appreciation of them. It does not come from our work but from our attitude toward our work. It does not come from success but from the growth we retain in achieving that success.

6. Spend time in peaceful thoughts.

7. No man can be happy who does not think himself so.

8. Happy are those who long to be just and good, for they shall be completely satisfied.

9. Half the world is on the wrong scent in the pursuit of happiness. They think it consists of having and getting. On the contrary, <u>it consists of giving and serving.</u>

10. Happy is the generous man.

11. A happy heart makes a cheerful face.

12. Surely, goodness and mercy shall follow me all the days of my life.

Eldon Bollinger

Romans 8:38–39 (ASV) will help our hearts now. This is the climax of his redemption teaching; [38]-*"For I am persuaded that neither death, nor life, nor angels, nor principalities, nor things present, nor things to come, nor powers,* [39]-*nor height, nor depth, nor any other creature, shall be able to separate us from the love of God, which is in Christ Jesus our Lord."*

He covers everything that can come to a man, every calamity that can possibly come in our earth walk, and tells us that none can separate us from the love of our Father.   In **Romans 8:35 (KJV)** we read, *"Who can separate us from the love of Christ?"*   <u>Nothing can separate us from the love of Christ nor from the Father's love. Nothing can do it. Know this! Let this be the background of your faith!</u>

ELDON'S PROVERBS AND MEMORY VERSES

KINDNESS 5:   REAL RICHES

1. And all the children shall be taught of the Lord; and great shall be the peace of thy children.   In righteousness shall they be established. That should

be far from oppression; for thou shall not fear and from terror, for it shall not come near.

2. Kindness gives birth to kindness.

3. A kind man benefits himself, but the cruel man brings trouble upon himself.

4. The rewards of kindness are great and the cost is so very little.

5. A kind person is like a rose in a garden of weeds.

6. <u>Be kind, for everyone you meet is fighting a battle.</u>

7. Kindness is a golden chain that binds society together.

8. Be kind to unkind people. They're probably hurting and miserable.

9. Kind words produce healing.

10. Kindness is poetry of the heart.

11. Gestures of kindness cost so little yet give great dividends to both the giver and the receiver.

Eldon Bollinger

CHAPTER 39

PROSPERITY

Prosperity is God's way and will always be the result of a life committed and dedicated and in line with God's Word. God wants you to have everything you need, but he does not want riches to have you.

"But thou shall remember the Lord thy God; for it is he that giveth thee power to get wealth, that he may establish his covenant"—**Deuteronomy 8:18 (KJV)**.

Remember, the purpose of this wealth is to establish his covenant. What is included in the covenant? It includes telling others the good news (the gospel), teaching them that God provides for his children.

<u>It means happiness, health, and prosperity in every way and in every area of your lives; this includes our marriages, our children, our bodies, our business, and our work or ministries.</u>

CHAPTER 40

HANG-UPS–ROADBLOCKS

Many people cannot achieve success because of their hang-ups, guilt, bad teachings, and more. Do not let "I can't" words come out of your mouth.

You are a son or daughter of God, so you are blessed with faithful Abraham; you can do all things through Christ! Get rid of the roadblocks.

ELDON'S PROVERBS AND MEMORY VERSES

KINDNESS 8:　　　REAL RICHES

1. In a world of pushing and shoving, grabbing and taking, a kind and giving person is like a beacon that everyone sees and are blessed thereby.

2. The Lord is gracious and merciful, slow to anger, and of great kindness.

3. God said, "With everlasting kindness will I have mercy on thee"—**Isaiah 54:8 (KJV)**.

4. Most people are kind to their friends and those who are kind to them, but it takes a real Christian to be kind to those who are unkind to you.

5. You may say you love others, but the way you live and the things you do will tell the real story.

6. The sweet fragrance of a kind and loving person lingers many years after he or she is gone.

7. <u>The wonderful memory of my mother, always loving, always giving, and always caring, regardless of what I had done, will follow me to my final resting place.</u>

8. God's great kindness and mercy. Oh, my people, with great compassion I will gather you. The mountains may depart and the hills disappear, but my kindness shall not leave you. My promise of peace for you will never be broken. Your people shall be taught by me and their prosperity shall be great. You will live under a government that is just and fair.

Eldon Bollinger

CHAPTER 41

PROSPERITY PLEASES GOD

"Let them shout for joy, and be glad, that favor my righteous cause: yea, let them say continually, Let the Lord be magnified, <u>which hath pleasure in the prosperity of his servant</u>"—(**Psalm 35:27 (KJV)**).   If God has pleasure in our prosperity, he must have displeasure in our poverty.

Many people have closed minds regarding the subject of success and prosperity. It is sad to see them cheated out of all that God wants them to have, yet they don't even realize they are the problem. Until the roadblocks are removed, those people will never be able to move into God's river of blessings.

[18-]*"Come now and let us reason together, saith the Lord; though your sins be as scarlet, they shall be as white as snow; though they be read like crimson, they shall be as wool.* [19-]*<u>If ye be willing and obedient, ye shall eat the good of the land</u>"*—**Isaiah 1:18–19 (KJV)**.

[10-]*"Say ye to the righteous, it shall be well with them: for they shall eat the fruit of their doings.* [11-]*Woe unto the*

wicked! It shall be ill with him: for the reward of his hand shall be given unto him"—**Isaiah 3:10–11 (KJV)**. You reap what so ever you sow!

Proverbs tells us *"...the way of the transgressor is hard"*—**Proverbs 13:15 (KJV)**!

"My people are destroyed for lack of knowledge..."—**Hosea 4:6 (KJV)**.

"My people have gone into captivity, because they have no knowledge"—**Isaiah 5:13 (KJV)**.

"Beloved, I wish above all things, that thou mayest prosper and be in health, even as thy soul prospers"—**3 John 1:2 (KJV)**.

"The fear of the wicked, it should come up on him: but the desire of the righteous shall be granted"—**Proverbs 10:24 (KJV)**!

<u>Above all things, God not only wishes that we may prosper and be in health even as our soul prospers. He also has pleasure in our prosperity! And if we are willing and obedient, we will eat the good of the land.</u>

"The Lord will perfect that which concerneth me..."—**Psalm 138:8 (KJV)**.

"A good man leaveth an inheritance to his children's children: and the wealth of the sinner is laid up for the just"—**Proverbs 13:22 (KJV)**.

"The Lord's blessing is our greatest wealth, all our work adds nothing to it"—**Proverbs 10:22 (LB)**.

"Wickedness never brings real success; only the godly have that"—**Proverbs 12:3 (LB)**!

3- *"According, as his divine power hath given unto us all things that pertain unto life and godliness, through the knowledge of him that has called us to glory and virtue:* **4-** *Whereby are given unto us exceeding great and precious promises: that by these ye might be partakers of the divine nature..."*—**2 Peter 1:3–4 (KJV)**.

"For if by one man's offence death reigned by one; much more they which receive abundance of grace and the gift of righteousness, shall reign in life by one Jesus Christ"—**Romans 5:17 (KJV)**.

"For we know that all things work together for good to them that love God, to them who are called according to his purpose"—**Romans 8:28 (KJV)**.

"And God is able to make all grace abound toward you: that ye, always have all sufficiency in all things, may abound to every good work"—**2 Corinthians 9:8 (KJV)**.

We are made overcomers by the blood of the Lamb (Jesus) and by the Word of our testimony.

God is our Father, we are his children; we are in his family; we not only must know this in our hearts, but it will never be a reality until we confess it with our mouth.

"Watch and pray always that you may be accounted worthy to escape <u>all</u>..."—**Luke 21:36 (KJV)**.

Are you ready for our Lord's return, and are you living a life before God that is acceptable to him? Are you looking for his return? There will be many who are not ready and will miss the rapture.

CHAPTER 42

THE FOOLISH VIRGINS
AND LUKEWARM CHRISTIANS

1-"Then shall the kingdom of heaven be likened unto ten virgins, which took their lamps, and went forth to meet the bridegroom. 2-And five of them were wise, and five were foolish. 3-They that were foolish took their lamps, and took no oil with them: 4-but the wise took oil in their vessels with their lamps. 5-While the bridegroom tarried, they all slumbered and slept. 6-And at midnight there was a cry made: "Behold, the bridegroom cometh; go ye out to meet him." 7-Then all those virgins arose, and trimmed their lamps. 8-And the foolish said unto the wise, 'Give us of your oil; for our lamps are gone out.' 9-But the wise answered, saying, 'Not so; lest there be not enough for us and you: but go ye rather to them that sell, and buy for yourselves.' 10-And while they went to buy, the bridegroom came; and they that were ready went in with him to the marriage: and the door was shut. 11-Afterward came also the other virgins, saying, 'Lord, Lord, open to us.' 12-But he answered and said, 'Verily I say unto you, I know you not. 13-Watch therefore, for ye know neither the day nor the hour wherein the Son of man cometh'"—**Matthew 25:1–13 (KJV).** The foolish virgins will miss the rapture!

I believe there are many Christians who have not cleaned up this old body and are not really walking with God, they are like the five foolish virgins; I believe they will miss the rapture and have to go through at least the first half of the seven-year tribulation period.

Revelation describes this group at mid-tribulation time.

[9]-*"After this I beheld, and, lo, a great multitude, which no man could number, of all nations, and kindred's, and people, and tongues, stood before the throne, and before the Lamb, clothed with white robes, and palms in their hands;* [10]-*and cried with a loud voice, saying, Salvation to our God which sitteth upon the throne, and unto the Lamb.* [11]-*And all the angels stood round about the throne, and about the elders and the four beasts, and fell before the throne on their faces, and worshipped God,* [12]-*Saying, Amen: Blessing, and glory, and wisdom, and thanksgiving, and honor, and power, and might, be unto our God forever and ever. Amen.* [13]-*And one of the elders answered, saying unto me, what are these which are arrayed in white robes? And whence came they? And* [14]-*I said unto him, Sir, thou knowest. And he said to me, these are they which came out of great tribulation, and have washed their robes, and made them white in the blood of the Lamb"*—**Revelation 7:9–14 (KJV).**

[21]-"Not everyone that saith unto me, Lord, Lord, shall enter into the kingdom of heaven; but he that doeth the will of my Father which is heaven. [22]-Many will say to me in that day, 'Lord, Lord, have we not prophesied in thy name? and in thy name have cast out devils? and in thy name done many wonderful works?' [23]-And then will I profess unto them, 'I never knew you: depart from me, ye that work iniquity'"—**Matthew 7:21–23 (KJV)**.

"Watch ye therefore, and pray always, that ye may be accounted worthy to escape all these things that shall come to pass, and to stand before the Son of man"—**Luke 21:36 (KJV)**.

[1]-*"But of the times and the seasons, brethren, ye have no need that I write unto you. [2]-For yourselves know perfectly that the day of the Lord so cometh as a thief in the night. [3]-For when they shall say, Peace and safety; then sudden destruction cometh upon them, as travail upon a woman with child; and they shall not escape. [4]-But ye, brethren, are not in darkness, that that day should overtake you as a thief. [5]-Ye are all the children of light, and the children of the day: we are not of the night, nor of darkness. [6]-Therefore let us not sleep, as do others; but let us watch and be sober. [7]-For they that sleep, sleep in the night; and they that be drunken are drunken in the night. [8]-But let us, who are of the day, be sober, putting on the breastplate of faith and love; and for an helmet, the hope of salvation. [9]-For God hath not appointed us to wrath, but to obtain salvation by our Lord Jesus Christ"*—**1 Thessalonians 5:1–9 (KJV)**. Christians are not appointed to the time of God's great wrath.

ELDON'S PROVERBS AND MEMORY VERSES

KINDNESS 1:   REAL RICHES

1. Kind words can be short and easy to speak, but their echoes are truly endless.

2. Kindness is a language the deaf can hear and the blind can see.

3. Kindness is the oil that takes the friction out of life.

4. Be kind to unkind people; they probably need it the most.

5. The Lord is gracious and merciful, slow to anger, and of great kindness.

6. Kind words are like honey, enjoyable and healthful.

7. One of the fruits of the spirit is kindness.

8. One can pay back a loan, but you are forever indebted to those who are kind.

9. Remember that everyone is influenced by kindness.

10. Kindness makes a man's face attractive.

11. Kindness should become the Christian's way of life.

12. Kindness begets kindness and happiness always follows a kind person.

Eldon Bollinger

CHAPTER 43

YOUR FUTURE IS UNLIMITED

When you fully realize you are a child of God, that you are an heir and joint heir with Jesus Christ and that God is your heavenly Father, it shouldn't surprise you that God created you for success and that he laid out great plans for your life. When this registers in your spirit, it becomes easy to believe God for great and mighty things. It becomes easy to believe God's favor is upon your life and he wants good things for you, just as if you want good things for your children.

You need to expect great things, get a bigger vision for your life. Jesus said <u>according to your faith be it unto you,</u> begin to believe in favor everywhere you go, the right people to come into your life, the breaks you need in business. As you live in faith, nobody can keep you from your destiny–except you. Without a goal, people perish.

We will receive in this life what we really believe in and expect, and our faith is activated by what we say. Therefore, we need to not only expect and believe for great things and great blessing from God, we need to speak it.

Success comes as you meditate and speak God's Word. You are the one who determines your success in life. Giving God's Word first place in your life builds a shield of faith around you. Speaking faith-filled words attract God's blessings to you the same way a magnet draws metal to it.

The words you speak are powerful! They can be healing forces. They can minister life or death to you!

CHAPTER 44

LEARN TO SPEAK GOD'S WORD

[20] *"My son, attend to my words; incline thine ear unto my sayings.* [21] *Let them not depart from thine eyes; keep them in the midst of thine heart.* [22] *For <u>my words</u> are life unto those that find them, and health to all their flesh"*—**Proverbs 4:20–22 (KJV).**

ELDON'S PROVERBS AND MEMORY VERSES

ENTHUSIASM 1:   REAL RICHES

1. <u>Enthusiasm makes ordinary people extraordinary.</u>

2. Nothing great was ever accomplished without enthusiasm.

3. Enthusiasm is one of the most powerful engines of success. When you do a thing, do it with all your might. Put your whole self into it. Be active, be energetic, be enthusiastic, and be faithful, and you will accomplish your objective.

4. <u>When a person loves and gives, helps and serves, joy deepens and enthusiasm for God's world and its people measurably increase!</u>

5. <u>Fill your life with contagious enthusiasm.</u>

6. <u>Enthusiasm is by far the highest paid quality on earth.</u>

7. Every man is enthusiastic at times. One man has enthusiasm for thirty minutes. Another has it for thirty days–but the one who has it for thirty years is the one that makes a success of life.

8. If you lose everything but enthusiasm, you will yet succeed.

9. Get all excited and believe. All things are possible to him who believes.

10. Possess contagious enthusiasm.

11. Enthusiasm is one of life's greatest qualities.

12. Force yourself to act enthusiastic.

13. God's Word ministers to the total man. His Word is our wisdom, righteousness, sanctification, and redemption.

14. <u>The words we spoke in the past have made life what it is today.</u>

15. <u>The words we speak today will determine what our life will be like in the future.</u>

Eldon Bollinger

"Thou art snared with the words of thy mouth, thou art taken with the words of thy mouth"—**Proverbs 6:2 (KJV).**

Whatever we speak eventually becomes part of us and will control our life.

<u>Christ has redeemed me from the curse of the law. Therefore, I forbid any sickness or disease to come upon my body. Every disease germ and every virus that touches my body dies instantly, in the name of Jesus. Every organ and every tissue in my body functions in the perfection to which God created it to function and I forbid any malfunction in my body in Jesus name.</u> (See **Galatians 3:13, Romans 8:11, Genesis 1:31, & Matthew 16:19**).

<u>Christ hath redeemed me from the curse of the law. Therefore I am blessed in the city, I'm blessed in the field, I am blessed when I come in and I am blessed when I go out. For the Lord has commanded the blessing upon me in my storehouse, and in all that I set my hand unto.</u> (See **Galatians 3:13, & Deuteronomy 28**)!

The Lord became poor, that through his poverty I might be rich, see **2 Corinthians 8:9.**

188

I do love the Lord and he gives me the desires of my heart, see **Psalm 37:4**.

I have given cheerfully and my God has made all grace abound to me and I have all sufficiency in all things and I do abound in good works, see **2 Corinthians 9:6–8**.

ELDON'S PROVERBS AND MEMORY VERSES

PROSPERITY 2:   REAL RICHES

1. God's prosperity blesses many.

2. Strong men retain riches.

3. God's blessing is our greatest wealth.

4. Enter-God's rest **[Hebrews 4:9]** and prosperity always follows.

5. A man who receives prosperity from God will always bless those around him.

6. There is no want for those who follow God's path.

7. God's prosperity blesses many.

8. God has touched the lives of those who are truly rich.

9. Remember the Lord thy God, for it is he who giveth thee power to obtain wealth.

10. Prosperity pleases God.

11. The blessing of the Lord–it maketh rich and it addith no sorrow with it.

Eldon Bollinger

<u>I have no lack, "For my God shall supply all my needs according to his riches in glory by Christ Jesus"</u>—**Philippians 4:19 (KJV).**

<u>Jesus came that I might have life and that I might have it more abundantly,</u> see **John 10:10**.

It doesn't matter where you are in life; there are exciting things in your future if you will just believe. This is a new day; this is your day for a new beginning. I know God has great moments of favor coming your way! Let me encourage you: God has ordained great things in your future. He has them planned out for you. You may have so much clutter in your life that you can't hear the still, small voice inside you: but if you will believe, your moment of favor is here.

We often become frustrated when things don't come to pass as quickly as we think they should. Be patient. Trust God.

Let me give you an example of how I believe God wants to work in our lives.

On September 15, 2010, my partner, Bob Weatherford, and I went to our office knowing the quarterly report to the government was due and had to be paid that day. It was Friday, and our five workers had to be paid. We needed several thousand dollars, and our money had not come in as we'd expected. The company account showed less than two hundred dollars, and mine and Bob's personal accounts both contained little funds. We needed a miracle, and praise God, we got one! A couple came into the office and wanted to buy a property that had been on the market for several months. They wanted to pay sixteen thousand dollars down and the balance in about six months. We closed the transaction within a few hours, and there was plenty of money to go around and an overflow. A real estate transaction never closes within a few hours. Only God can do something like that.

That wasn't a lucky break. That was God bringing things together for us. That's why we don't have to worry. We don't have to go around frustrated and fearful because things aren't happening as fast as we would like. All we have to do is stay in faith, knowing God is directing our steps. As long as we keep believing, our moments of favor are here.

Get this straight in your spirit: God has already lined up favor for you–the right people, the right breaks, the right opportunities. He prearranged them for your future. That's the way God is. The Scriptures say [**1 Corinthians 2:9**] that no man has ever seen, heard, or imagined the wonderful things God has in store for us.

You may think, "I have really messed my life up, there's no hope," but that's not true. Where you are today is no surprise to God. He's not up in heaven all baffled, thinking, *Man, I never knew he'd get that far off track. I didn't know he'd blow it that bad.* No, God knew you would be where you are and what you would be before he formed the earth and all the fullness thereof. He's already filled your future opportunities with mercy and restoration. The fact is, God has solutions to problems you haven't even encountered yet.

I wish I could fully explain the love God has for his children and the beautiful things he has planned for you. Things he spoke into existence for all of us. **1 Corinthians 2:9** says, "Eye hath not seen, ear hath not heard, neither hath entered into the hearts of man those things which God has prepared for those who love him." There are plans for your happiness, laughter, joy, and peace, and although the world is raging, he gives us peace and an assurance that all is well.

2 Timothy 3:1 (KJV) tells us "…that in the last days, perilous times shall come." We are not to fear because God is our protector, and he says that no evil can befall those who trust him. But there is great peace for the man of God who trusts God completely, for we know the rapture is at hand.

Luke 21:36 tells us to watch and pray always that we may be accounted worthy to escape all. Yes, the world may be raging, but Jesus said he will prepare a place for us, and if he prepares a place, he will come again and receive us. Yes, we are living in the end times, and Jesus said he will come again for those who are looking for his return.

I may not be able to express it as I feel it, but I want you to fully understand how much God loves you and wants the very best for each of his children. I want you to understand how much I love you and want the very best for each of you who undertakes these studies–please believe.

ELDON'S PROVERBS AND MEMORY VERSES

JOY 6: REAL RICHES

1. <u>We have a choice:</u> you can choose to be happy, with joy, or you can let the cares of this life and the problems you face make you unhappy, bitter, resentful, and critical. If you choose the latter, Satan will have you defeated.

2. Choose God's way: let the joy of the Lord be your strength.

3. So shall my Word be that goeth forth out of my mouth: it shall not return me void, but it shall accomplish that which I please and shall prosper in the thing where to I send it. Let the joy of the Lord rule your life and his blessings will always follow.

4. Joy is the best therapy there is.

5. Every morning declare the joy of the Lord your strength.

6. Happiness is the result of circumstances, but joy endures in spite of circumstances.

7. The earth breaks forth in praise to God and sings for utter joy.

8. In thy presence is joy and at the right hand there are pleasures forevermore.

9. A joyful person brings happiness to everyone around him or her–be that person.

Eldon Bollinger

CHAPTER 45

YOUR DAY OF VICTORY IS COMING 2

When they crucified Jesus, it was a dark day, probably the most painfully discouraging day of his life. In fact, it was so bad, Jesus earlier sweat great drops of blood. It probably looked like his life was over. Most people thought his enemies had finished him. But, God had other plans. Although they put his body in a grave, three days later, he arose victorious.

Death could not keep him in the grave. The forces of darkness could not stop him. On the third day, Jesus came out of the grave and said, "I was dead, but now I am alive forevermore." No matter how dark it looks, no matter how long it has been, no matter how many people are trying to push us down, if we stay in faith, God will turn things around for us.

You may have problems in your path. You can't see how you can never accomplish your dreams, or how you can recover your health, or resolve your problems. Negative thoughts are bombarding you: it may seem to be all over, that it will never be any better. But, God has the final say! God's Word declares that all things work together for good to those who love God and are called according to his purpose. <u>God has the final say and your day of victory is coming.</u>

When God put those dreams in your heart, he made plans to see them fulfilled. The good news is he already has a completion date for them. You may not see how that could happen. It may be taking a long time. The odds appear to be against you. However, if you just keep believing, keep praying, and keep being your best, God will cause those dreams to become a reality. <u>Your day of victory is on its way.</u>

Although problems might look overwhelming, God is not limited by things. He's got resurrection power; he can give you one break that will put you on a new level of life. He can open doors that no man can shut. He can bring talent out of you that you didn't know you had. He can send people who will go out of their way to be good to you.

Just keep believing and praying and you will come into your supernatural increase. When your path seems darkest, you feel lost and defeated, so make a declaration of faith and declare, "I know my day of victory is almost here!" What you're really saying is, "God, I know you will turn this situation around, and I know you will heal my body or meet whatever need I have."

Don't be discouraged and complain; speak to the problem and speak victory over your circumstances. **Philippians 1:6** states that <u>God will bring you to a</u>

<u>flourishing finish.</u> Therefore, God will finish what he started with you, and it will turn out bigger and better than you ever imagined. Just stay in faith and be the person you know God wants you to be. Whatever your dream, the good news is, God already has a completion date for you.

The prophet Elisha was promised a double portion of Elijah's anointing. In the Scripture, there are seven major miracles attributed to Elijah. That means Elisha should have experience fourteen miracles. Elisha found himself on his deathbed after experiencing only thirteen miracles. He was one short of the promised allotment; with that in mind, Elisha probably hoped reports of his impending death were exaggerated. After all, he knew God is a God of completion.

Still, God works according to his own plan. With just thirteen miracles on his record, Elisha died! Surprised family then placed him in an open grave.

Elisha was still in the open grave when along came a group of people carrying a man killed in battle. They were in a hurry, so they decided to put his body in with Elisha's. They lowered him in, and when his body touched Elisha's, he came back to life. He stood up and walked out of the grave!

God came through when it counted most, and that was miracle number fourteen! That tells me that as long as we stay in faith, as long as we keep believing, every promise

God puts in our hearts will come to pass. Not even death can keep God from bring it to completion.

When you are tempted to get discouraged, just turn it around and say, "Father, I want to thank you that you finish what you started in my life. I know you are God of completion."

Remember, it's not by our own might or power that our lives are completed. We reach fulfillment when God releases his favor into our dreams, so hold fast to what God put in your heart. Stay determined and go out each day in faith and expectancy.

You may have a future filled with hope, faith, blessing, and promotion. If you are impatient, you may become discouraged. You may feel frustrated, maybe even tempted to make bad decisions, but let me remind you who you are and what you have on the inside. You are a child of the Most High God. You have seeds of greatness inside you. You have royal blood flowing through your veins. You have been crowned with glory and honor. You are destined to leave your mark on this generation. It may not have happened yet, but the promise is still in you. Don't give up on your future. Don't make decisions that you will regret. Let me assure you that great days lie ahead. You will see your dreams come to pass. When it's time for God to promote you, to vindicate you, to restore you, all the forces of darkness cannot stop good things from happening.

You may feel frustrated now, but God is working behind the scene in your life and is arranging the right breaks, the right people, and the right opportunities. Sometimes the process takes longer before all of the pieces are in place. Patience is critical. **Psalm 106** warns that the people of Israel did not wait for God's plan to unfold. They missed their promised land because they became discouraged. They complained and gave up hope. Don't let this happen to you. Stay in faith. Recognize that God may be testing you. If you let his plan unfold, you'll find that God will give you something better than you dreamed.

When is God's appointed time? God knows when the time is correct. When you understand this principle, it takes the pressure off. It's a stress-free way to live, knowing that as long as we stay in faith, God will release his favor, his restoration, his healing at exactly the right time in our lives. Just stay in faith knowing that God will bring your promise to pass, and he will bring it to a flourishing finish! It's time for your restoration. Your best is yet to come!

"For if by one man's offence death reigned by one; much more they which receive abundance of grace and of the gift of righteousness <u>shall reign in life by one, Jesus Christ"</u>—**Romans 5:17 (KJV)**.

Do you reign your life?

CHAPTER 46

GOD'S ABUNDANT PROVISION

God wants to give you abundant provision; he wants to give you the desires of your heart. I believe that even right now, because you're in faith, because you're saying, "Lord, I believe," he is arranging things in your favor. He is lining up the right people, the right opportunities.

In the days and weeks ahead, you will see supernatural increase, explosive blessings. God will give you the desires of your heart. New might as well get ready. God has some mighty blessings coming your way. You are headed for supernatural increase, supernatural healing, and supernatural restoration. God wants to utterly amaze you with his goodness and kindness!

There are at least two important scriptural facts related to being productive, or to bearing fruit. I believe these two facts will create in you the faith you need to be fully productive.

ELDON'S PROVERBS AND MEMORY VERSES

HAPPINESS 4:   REAL RICHES

1. Most people are as happy as they make up their minds to be.

2. Happiness is a perfume you cannot pour on others without getting a few drops on yourself.

3. <u>Live happily with the wife you love through the fleeting days of life, for the wife God gives you is your best reward down here for all your earthly toil.</u>

4. What happiness for those whose guilt has been forgiven! What joy when sins are covered over! What relief for those who have confessed their sins and God has cleared their record.

5. This is the day the Lord has made: we will rejoice and be glad therein.

6. Make every day useful, cheerful, and happy.

7. Faith, love, peace, and hope make your life one of happiness.

8. Laugh at yourself and pray for others.

9. Drive out thoughts of fear, discouragement, and unhappiness.

10. Expect the best and you will attain your heart's desire.

11. I have set the Lord always before me: because he is at my right hand, I shall not be moved. He will show me the path of life: in his presence is the fullness of joy.

12. Laughter is a tranquilizer with no side effects.

Eldon Bollinger

The first fact is this: God wants us to be fruitful. This is a settled matter of the will of God. It is not something that is going to change. It is true right from God's creation of man. It was the very purpose for which he created man. This is settled in **Genesis 1: 27–28 (KJV)** where we read an account of God's creation of man and the purpose for which he created him; [27]-*"So God created man in his own image, in the image of God created he him; male and female created he them. [28]-And God blessed them, and God said unto them, 'Be fruitful, and multiply, and replenish the earth, and subdue it: and have dominion over the fish of the sea, and over the fowl of the air, and over every living thing that moveth upon the earth.'"*

In these scriptures, God instructed us that he wanted man to do five things.

1. To be fruitful

2. To increase in number

3. To fill the earth

4. To subdue the earth

5. To rule over the fish of the sea and the birds of the air and over every living creature that moves on the ground.

These are the purposes for which man was created. God's purposes never change. Their fulfillment may be delayed by man's failure, but ultimately, God is always going to achieve his purposes.

In the new creation, in Jesus Christ, the same purposes of God are restored once again. This is made clear in many places in the New Testament, and one in particular. There is a prayer of the apostle Paul for the Christians with whom he was dealing.

The beautiful prayer is recorded in **Colossians 1:9–12 (NIV)** and has an entirely positive emphasis, [9]-"For this reason, since the day we heard about you, we have not stopped praying for you and asking God to fill you with the knowledge of his will through all spiritual wisdom and understanding. [10]-And we pray this in order that you may live a life worthy of the Lord and may please him in every way: bearing fruit in every good work, growing in the knowledge of God, [11]-being strengthened with all power according to His glorious might so that you may have great endurance and patience, and enjoy fullness: [12]-giving thanks to the Father, who has qualified you to share in the inheritance of the saints in the kingdom of light.

Let me point out all the positive words in this passage. First, Paul speaks about the Christians at Colosse being filled with the knowledge of God's will—not just having somewhere in them the knowledge of God's will but being filled with it. This comes from all *spiritual wisdom and understanding* (**Colossians 1:9**).

Then he prayed that they may live a life pleasing to the Lord in every way—not just pleasing him in some ways but pleasing him in every way. And he prayed that they may bear fruit in every good work. **Colossians 1:10**: that is the hundredfold Christian growing in the knowledge of God.

Then he prayed they may be strengthened with all power according to his glorious might. **Colossians 1:11** not some power, but all power—with the result that they may have great endurance.

Perseverance or endurance was one of the keywords in the parable of the sower. Here, Paul wants us to have great endurance and patience and joy. Finally, Paul uses the statement that God the Father has qualified us to share in the inheritance of the saints in the kingdom of light,

Colossians 1:12. <u>God has given us the provision that is needed to enter into our inheritance in the kingdom of light.</u>

God's will is settled forever in the Word of God. He wants us to be fruitful; he wants us to bear fruit, to succeed in every good work, and to please him in every way. He has also qualified us, or equipped us, to do this.

We have seen already that God wants us to be fruitful in every good work. This is the will of God. There is no question about his will—<u>the question is our response to his will.</u>

CHAPTER 47

GOD HAS MADE FULL PROVISION

The fact is this: God has made full provisions for us so we might be fruitful. We have seen from Paul's prayer that God has equipped us, or qualified us, to take our place in the inheritance of the saints in the kingdom of light. This truth is brought out in many ways in the New Testament.

Here is a very powerful statement that God has made full provision for this! 3-*"According as his divine power hath given unto us all things that pertain unto life and godliness, through the knowledge of him that hath called us to glory and virtue:* 4-*Whereby are given unto us exceeding great and precious promises: that by these ye might be partakers of the divine nature, having escaped the corruption that is in the world through lust"*—**2 Peter 1:3–4(KJV).**

Notice that opening phrase: his divine power. That's total omnipotence. His unlimited power has given us everything we need. Let me emphasize that God has given us everything we need for life and godliness. That is provided in two related ways: first, through our knowledge of him who called us, <u>that is, through the knowledge of Jesus Christ; and second, through his very great and precious promises.</u> The provision comes through knowing Jesus Christ <u>and through appropriating the promises of God's Word.</u>

There is a saying: The provision in the promises of God's Word is contained in all the provision we will ever need. You might say God has given us full provision–so where is it? <u>The answer is that it is in the promises of God's Word. As you appropriate these promises, you discover the provision.</u>

<u>There are two marvelous results of appropriating the promise. The first is that we participate in the divine nature. The very nature of God himself comes into us as we begin to share in his divine nature. Second, the logical negative consequence is that we escape the corruption that is in the world caused by evil desires. How do you feel about the possibility of becoming a partaker of God's own nature and escaping the corruption that is in the world through evil desires? Does that not appeal to you? God has made full provision for that. He has made it possible for you and me to do that. Everything we need is already been given to us.</u>

CHAPTER 48

ENTHUSIASM

Keep the magic of enthusiasm working for you. The Greek word for enthusiasm means "God within" or "God filled." There is magic in enthusiasm. I want this chapter to forever change your life. Enthusiasm is contagious, and I hope you catch it. It is not only contagious but infectious, stimulating, and attractive to others. Enthusiasm is wonderful and is life changing for you and everyone around you.

You have the choice, so choose to be enthusiastic today. Practice joyful, happy enthusiasm today. Give thanks and praise for your blessings today. Do something today to make someone else happy. Develop the habit of thinking happy thoughts. Choose to be happy, enthusiastic, and joyful all day, every day; the choice is yours.

A world of joyfulness and enthusiasm, of delight and wonder is all about us. Can you not see that it is God filled and God has prepared it for his children? Oh the joy for those who are allowed to see the wonders of God's creation. Rejoice and be exceedingly glad, become enthusiastic and joyful, turn your faith loose, and rise to new levels in your faith walk with God. Happiness, joy, and peace will always follow. God prepared all things just for his family, and we must rejoice and be exceedingly glad.

Happiness, joy, and enthusiasm are a choice. Realize that this day is a gift from God and you have the choice to be happy with enthusiasm and joy or unhappy with discouragement. All the negative things Satan can put in my mind. I choose happiness, joy, and enthusiasm. We need to realize that the world is filled with beauty and excitement. Keep yourself sensitive to it. Love the world and its people. I believe that anyone trying consistently to follow that simple advice will have a life full of enthusiasm and great joy.

The person who loves will eventually become enthusiastic. If you are not enthusiastic, deliberately begin today to cultivate the love of living.

Attitudes are more important than facts. Enthusiasm often helps work what people describe as miracles in solving problems. This is because enthusiasm is an attitude of the mind, and the mental attitude in a difficult situation is an important factor in its solution. Indeed, attitudes are more important than facts, for enthusiasm changes the mental outlook from fearing facts to a solid assurance that there is an answer.

Enthusiasm, like mumps, measles, and the common cold, is highly contagious. But, unlike measles, mumps, and colds, enthusiasm is good for you. I hope you catch it.

When you're contagious and enthusiastic, faith in yourself sets you free from the self-made prison of your mind. You will begin to change, and as you change, your whole life changes. You will be set free to live on a level that you have never experienced before. Enthusiasm will help your faith build, and the Lord will help you turn things around.   Your victories will fill you with enthusiasm and joy. The problems will give way before enthusiasm and joy and positive faith and you will become a victor, a conqueror, and an overcomer.

Study and meditate on God's Word and it will activate your mind so that it becomes alive and vital. Pay attention to the Bible, which tells us to walk in newness of life. That is a powerful thought. We are not to think old, dead, lifeless thoughts. Walk in newness of life, in the quality of life that is new every morning and fresh every morning, always exciting and joyful.

The Bible is filled with excitement and enthusiasm. It is well called the book of life. And we are to be renewed in the spirit of our mind, not merely on the surface of your mind but in the deep spirit that activates your thoughts. Joy and enthusiasm can make your life rich and full, and this book will help you think and live the joy way, the enthusiastic way.

"For if by one man's offence death reigned by one; much more they which receive abundance of grace and of

the gift of righteousness shall reign in life by one, Jesus Christ"—**Romans 5:17 (KJV).**

"And be not conformed to this world: but be ye transformed by the renewing of your mind, that ye may prove what is that good, and acceptable, and perfect, will of God"—**Romans 12:2 (KJV).**

"Now the God of hope fill you with all joy and peace in believing, that ye may abound in hope, through the power of the Holy Ghost"—**Romans 15:13 (KJV).**

We are encouraged to study, read, and meditate on God's Word, for in this Word is life. By feeding upon it, we become conditioned with a spiritual uplift of joy, enthusiasm, and vitality of spirit that will produce in us a tide of spiritual power and thrust that will overflow our life with a spirit of success and victory.

ELDON'S PROVERBS AND MEMORY VERSES

ENTHUSIASM 1:   REAL RICHES

1. <u>Enthusiasm makes ordinary people extraordinary.</u>

2. Nothing great was ever accomplished without enthusiasm.

3. Enthusiasm is one of the most powerful engines of success. When you do a thing do it with your might. Put your whole self into it. Be active, be energetic,

be enthusiastic and faithful and you will accomplish your objective.

4. <u>When a person loves and gives, helps and serves, joy deepens and enthusiasm for God's world and its people measurably increase!</u>

5. <u>Fill your life with contagious enthusiasm.</u>

6. <u>Enthusiasm is by far the highest paid quality on earth.</u>

7. Every man is enthusiastic at times. One man has enthusiasm for thirty minutes. Another has it for thirty days–but the one that has it for thirty years is the one that makes a success of life.

8. If you lose everything but enthusiasm, you will yet succeed.

9. Get all excited, and believe. All things are possible to he who believes.

10. Possess contagious enthusiasm.

11. Enthusiasm is one of life's greatest qualities.

12. Force yourself to act enthusiastic.

Eldon Bollinger

The New Testament is filled to overflow with life (**John 1:4**). In Christ was life. When we center our life in Christ, the trash, the deadness, the gloom, the apprehension, the weariness, and the tiredness will disappear and a great inrush of joy and enthusiasm will follow. The joyous vitality of Christ will flood your life.

"The kingdom of God is within you"—**Luke 17:21 (KJV)**. Let it flow out, in your smile, in your activities with others, in everything that you do. Show forth God's love, God's peace, God's joy, and your enthusiasm for life.

<u>Make the decision right now that you will double the amount of enthusiasm that you have been putting into your work and into your life. If you actually do that, be prepared to see astonishing results. It will probably double your income and double your happiness.</u>

<u>If you can give your son or daughter only one gift, let it be enthusiasm!</u>

Frank Bettger says in his book *How I Raised Myself from Failure to Success in Selling,* "I firmly believe enthusiasm is by far the biggest single factor in successful selling. For example, I know a man who is an authority on insurance. He could write a book yet he can't make a decent living selling it. Largely because of a lack of enthusiasm. I know another man who didn't know one tenth as much about insurance, yet became rich and retired in twenty years. The reason for his success was not knowledge, it was enthusiasm he became a human dynamo, just by forcing himself to act enthusiastic."

Your life can be rich and overflowing with God's love and blessings. Learn today to seek first the kingdom of God and let him enrich your life.

[1]"Praise ye the LORD. Blessed *is* the man *that* feareth the LORD, *that* delighteth greatly in his commandments. [2]His seed [children] shall be mighty upon earth: the generation of the upright shall be blessed. [3]Wealth and riches *shall be* in his house: and his righteousness endureth forever"—**Psalm 112:1–3 (KJV)**.

ELDON'S PROVERBS AND MEMORY VERSES

HAPPINESS 6:   REAL RICHES

1. Just remember that the tea kettle, even though it's up to its neck in hot water, continues to sing.

2. Mothers who start the day with kindness and smiles and tender words have the happiest home.

3. A spoonful of happiness does more good than a spoonful of medicine.

4. We choose happiness.

5. A merry heart doeth good like a medicine.

6. A smiling salesperson has the deal half made.

7. Greater love hath no man than this that a man should lay down his life for a friend.

8. The voice is richer when blended with a smile.

9. We like to remember the glad face, the happy smile, and joyful words.

10. Most of us miss out on life's big prizes, such as the Nobel, the Oscar, the Tony and the Emmys. However, we are all eligible for life's small pleasures: a big hug, a pat on the back, a great meal, a beautiful sunset, and good friends. Enjoy life's little delights. There are plenty for all.

Eldon Bollinger

CHAPTER 49

HEAVEN SHALL BE WORTH IT ALL

[1]-"And I saw a new heaven and a new earth: for the first heaven and the first earth were passed away; and there was no more sea. [2]-And I John saw the holy city, new Jerusalem, coming down from God out of heaven, prepared as a bride adorned for her husband. [3]-And I heard a great voice out of heaven saying, Behold, the tabernacle of God is with men, and he will dwell with them, and they shall be his people, and God himself shall be with them, and be their God. [4]-And God shall wipe away all tears from their eyes; and there shall be no more death, neither sorrow, nor crying, neither shall there be any more pain: for the former things are passed away. [5]-And he that sat upon the throne said, Behold, I make all things new. And he said unto me, Write: for these words are true and faithful. [6]-And he said unto me, It is done. I am Alpha and Omega, the beginning and the end. I will give unto him that is athirst of the fountain of the water of life freely. [7]-He that overcometh shall inherit all things; and I will be his God, and he shall be my son. [8]-But the fearful, and unbelieving, and the abominable, and murderers, and whoremongers, and sorcerers, and idolaters, and all liars, shall have their part in the lake

which burneth with fire and brimstone: which is the second death"—**Revelation 21:1–8 (KJV).**

"But as it is written, Eye hath not seen, nor ear heard, neither have entered into the heart of man, the things which God hath prepared for them that love him"—**1 Corinthians 2:9 (KJV).**

[15]-"Therefore are they before the throne of God, and serve him day and night in his temple: and <u>he that sitteth on the throne shall dwell among them.</u> [16]-<u>They shall hunger no more, neither thirst anymore; neither shall the sun light on them, nor any heat.</u> [17]-<u>For the Lamb which is in the midst of the throne shall feed them, and shall lead them unto living fountains of waters: and God shall wipe away all tears from their eyes</u>"—**Revelation 7:15–17 (KJV).**

I pray that you all have been born into the family of God and have become sons and daughters of God, heirs of God, and joint heirs with Jesus Christ. I want to see you successful, victorious Christians, walking in the fullest of all God has for you while you are here on earth, here and now. I want to see you in heaven, enjoying the wonders of heaven, things that are so wonderful that you have never even imagined them. In addition, I want you to make the rapture and escape all that is coming up on this earth.

MY PRAYERS WILL ALWAYS BE WITH YOU!

GOD BLESS – GOD BLESS!

STUDIES BY DR. ELDON BOLLINGER
Great Commission Bible College
www.gcbcedu.us

1. THE BELIEVER'S NEW LIFE-BENE463–3 HRS.
2. THE DEEPER WALK-DEWA516–4 HRS.
3. THE DEEPER WALK-DEWA517–4 HRS.
4. END TIME EVENTS-ENTI458–8 HRS.
5. FAITH FOR TODAY-FAFO111–3 HRS.
6. FAITH FOR TODAY-FAFO112–5 HRS.
7. SUCCESS THRU THE SCRIPTURE-SUTH553–3 HRS.
8. TEACH ME TO PRAY-TEME512–4 HRS.
9. YOUR BEST IS YET TO COME-YOBE312–3 HRS.
10. YOUR BEST IS YET TO COME-YOBE313–3 HRS.
11. SANCTIFICATION-RIGHTEOUSNESS-HOLINESS-SARI412–3 HRS.
12. SANCTIFICATION-RIGHTEOUSNESS-HOLINESS-SARI413–3 HRS.
13. OUR FINAL GENERATION OUFI365–3 HRS.
14. JESUS 1-JESU125–3 HRS.
15. JESUS 2-JESU126–3 HRS.
16. ISRAEL'S FALL AND REDEMPTION-ISFA145–4 HRS.
17. REVELATION REVEALED ONE-RERE155–3 HRS.
18. REVELATION REVEALED TWO-RERE156–3 HRS.
19. THE AUTHORITY OF THE CHURCH-THAU257–3 HRS.
20. GOD'S PROTECTION PLAN FOR YOU.
21. WHAT ABOUT YOUR FUTURE?–E BOOK.
22. YOUR FUTURE GOD'S WAY–SERIES # 1–3 HRS.
23. YOUR FUTURE GOD'S WAY–SERIES # 2–3 HRS.
24. YOUR FUTURE GOD'S WAY–SERIES # 3–3 HRS.
25. OUR FINAL GENERATION–OUFI–3 HRS.

My Anointing and Spirit are on all of the above studies and will follow them wherever they go.

Eldon Bollinger

218

<u>References</u>

<u>Bibles</u>

Living Bible	(LB)
(New) King James Version	(KJV)-(NKJV)
New Living Translation	(NLT)
English Standard Version	(ESV)
New International Version	(NIV)
(New) American Standard Version	(ASV)-(NASV)

<u>Other Books By Dr. Eldon & Wanell Bollinger</u>

Jesus

Love

Our Final Generation

Prayer That Moves Mountains

Prophecy & End Time Events–Book 1

Prophecy & End Time Events–Book 2

Rise And Be Healed

Success Through God's Word

The Authority Of The Church

The Believer's New Life

What About Your Future? (This Book)

Without Holiness, No Man Shall See God

Your Best Is Yet To Come

Your Future God's Way

<u>Contact Us</u>

Like me on Facebook: http://www.facebook.com/eldon.bollinger

Eldon's e-Mail Address: eldonbollinger@gmail.com

One-Of-A-Kind Productions: www.ooakp.com

My Commission

God answered and said, "My son, just as I was with Jesus, so will I be with you. You go and cast out devils. You heal the sick. You cleanse the lepers. You raise the dead. I give you power over all the power of the enemy. Do not be afraid. Be strong. Be courageous. I am with you as I was with Jesus. No demon should be able to stand before you all the days of your life. I used men and women then, but now I desire to use you."

—January 7, 2012

This day will I begin to magnify you in the eyes of the people.

—*February 4, 2012*

[17]"O God, thou hast taught me from my youth: and hitherto have I declared thy wondrous works. [18]Now also when I am old and gray headed, O God, forsake me not; until I have showed thy strength unto *this* generation, *and* thy power to everyone *that* is to come."

—Psalm 71:17–18

Your greatest days are yet ahead, my son.

—January 13, 2013

Eldon Bollinger

Notes

221

Notes